Comments on Reading Virtual Minds Volumes I and II from Amazon.com

Insightful and surprisingly easy to read

I thought this book was going to be a daunting read (you know, the kind of book you have to sit in front of your computer with Google open and ready to look up everything), but it's not. The material, I will admit, is far more advanced than I usually read - but Joseph has this way of writing that makes even the most difficult of ideas easy to understand. I am a self-taught webmaster and I am always looking for new things to learn about web sites and how people view my site(s)...this book is sparking so many ideas of what I need to re-look at - and in a whole new way!

Inspiring from beginning to end!

Excellent, inspiring from a to z, and brought in such a comprehensible way even for the most complex concepts within this book series. It is actionable in its findings, great support for your marketing (or at least on how you could become more efficient and profitable in your marketing) thanks to this neurolinguistic marketing approach

This book addresses what marketers and designers need to attend ...

This book addresses what marketers and designers need to attend to create desired outcomes. And, how to decipher why desired outcomes were unattainable. Now, I need to start to incorporate more of those principles in my work.

This Book is the Zen and the Art of Motorcycle Maintenance for the 21st Century

I highly recommend this book to anyone who wants to grow as both a Leader and a Citizen of the World. As a Coast Guard Officer with assignments that include Training Officer and Navigator on board the CG Academy's Barque Eagle and Tactical Operations Center supervisor in the Port of Jebel Ali, U.A.E., I treasure this offering from Joseph for both it's leadership lessons - "behavior (is) the external demonstration of internal states" - and it's practical-individual application - "recognizing people through the sum of their parts is true even through machine interface. Recognizing individuals through a machine interface has been known since human-machine interfaces were first used..." (I didn't include the all-important footnote included in the book for even further exploration).

The first quote I gave, "behavior (is) the external demonstration of internal states" - when paired with other lessons I have been able to glean from this book - has inspired me to slow down and to listen to my subordinates. When you understand that human behavior - while it is often influenced by external factors - is solely based on what has been built over time within, you can better inspire your subordinates. For example, aligning personal goals with organizational goals.

The second quote "recognizing people through the sum of their parts is true even through machine interface. Recognizing individuals through a machine interface has been known since human-machine interfaces were first used..." reinforced the idea that we are individually unique: there is only one of us. And yet, each part of us can be categorized, which means we are not wholly unique. And meditating on that ambiguity, my friend, will lead you to a treasure trove of life lessons.

This is just a small part of the ways in which my personal filter was influenced while reading this. Not to mention included within is a pretty cool story of the development of an intelligent program. I like to think of it as a digital Anthropologist in the Field.

Through the teachings in his book and other publications, Joseph has taught me to better appreciate the hidden messages communicated by others in their body language, word choice, and emphasis. And he has taught me to better understand the messages I am communicating. And it is that unintentional communication that is always the most honest. If you want to better understand what people are communicating, if you need to have your message heard, I'd encourage you to read Joseph's work.

Reading Virtual Minds - A world-changing blend of 120 disciplines

Think of every science fiction movie and television show you've ever seen. Remember every scene where any physical object, from a robot to a chair, interacts with an individual according to their size, preferences, mood, etc.

Evolution Technology ("ET" for short), is the technology behind Reading Virtual Minds. The scenes you're remembering? ET makes them possible. All of them.

To sum up the book, "The human brain is wired in a specific way and is bound by the rules of that wiring. Anything which can't be attributed to direct cause and effect of that wiring must be unique to the individual using the computer [or any object]."

Age is unique.
Gender is unique.
Emotional engagement is unique.
Excitement is unique.
Frustration is unique.

Confusion is unique.

The threshold required to reach any of those emotional states is unique for each individual, and that barely scratches the surface. The list seems to be limited by the number of times someone asks "Can ET _____?".

The answer? Yes. It can. Further, Evolution technology is small, fast, and works with any human/object interface.

Re-stated so you don't miss that. It applies to -any human/object interface-.

- Education: Imagine being able to know the learning potential of any student in the classroom, and the moment any get confused.
- Education2: PCs (or iPads): Imagine eBooks that tailor themselves to the way your brain learns, so you can instantly recall what you read six months earlier.
- Human Resources/Management: Imagine live measurements of every departments' staff satisfaction level.
- Marketing: Imagine knowing which pages of your website bored your visitors before they decided to leave.
- Business: Imagine an alarm clock that reminds you of what you're doing every time you get distracted.
- Medical/Behavioral: Imagine diagnosing neurological & psychological disorders over the web.
- Automotive: Imagine your car recognizing you by touch, and your seats adjusting without controls until they sense you're comfortable.

Evolution Technology isn't just a dream. It's here. Today. Working. Many of my colleagues and I have used it and been amazed (and sometimes humbled) by the insights it provides.

New ET-based tools seem to pop up in the NextStage Knowledgeshop[a] every month - presents for the endlessly curious.

Like a cloud, ET has the potential to bring peaceful and refreshing mist, and it has the potential to bring oak-shattering lightning. NextStage tools' license agreements retain the right to refuse anyone in order to prevent harmful outcomes. Regardless of how it's used, however, Evolution Technology exists, and its existence will change your world.

As I said, I'm barely scratching the surface. Reading Virtual Minds, dimmed by its marketing-esque cover, heralds an age where our environment, our books, our possessions, understand what we need before we can ask for them. It also heralds an age of prejudices that have never before been possible. You owe it to yourself and those you care about to read it and explain it. I personally bought ten copies for family and friends.

Reading Joseph's Mind

I have been learning from Joseph in various ways for several years - sometimes in person, often through his writing. We have worked together on various projects together. His humor, stories and patience have been great aids to me as a novice in navigating social media in various forms. That humor, the story telling, insight and patience all come through in this book. It is not a "how-to," but rather an engaging introduction to his very original way of thinking about how individuals reveal themselves through their behaviors. My only critique is that at times I wish he had written a longer book: Some short paragraph would cause me to think about something in a new way and I wanted to explore what he meant and what I thought about it. Fortunately, he cross references his many writings elsewhere and promises a second volume. Through this book, I'm still learning from him, and that's the highest recommendation I can give anyone's (nonfiction) book.

––––––––––

[a] – Everything that was in the NextStage KnowledgeShop is now available to NextStage Members. See http://nlb.pub/4

(and)

Joseph is one of the best teachers I know ... particularly in his fields. Spending time with him through a book or in a class is a learning journey. He shows you things you didn't know you could know-about yourself and others, in your real and virtual lives. He's a true polymath bringing together many disciplines in new ways through his observations and the tools he creates to "see" others and ourselves in the on-line world. I recommend this book highly, but warn you that it is worth more than one reading!

Great neuroscience primer

Great read by the brilliant and ever irreverent Joseph Carrabis.

Reading Virtual Minds

Volume III: Fair-Exchange and Social Networks

Joseph Carrabis
Chief Research Officer & Founder
The NextStage Companies

First Edition Publication Oct 2016
Northern Lights Publishing
Nashua, NH, USA

Book cover, back cover photo and all logos by John Scullin –
http://www.skolenimation.com.

Reading Virtual Minds Volume III: Fair-Exchange and Social
Networks
1st Edition
all material copyright © 1999-2016 Joseph Carrabis.
All rights reserved.

Sections of this book were previously published on
The Hungry Peasant, http://www.hungrypeasant.com

ISBN: 978-0-9841403-6-7

It is the nature of men to be bound by the benefits they concur as much as by those they receive.
- Machiavelli, *The Prince*

Dedication

For Susan
ever patient, ever watchful, ever caring.

I can live in a universe with only her
but not in a universe without her.

Second to AJ
(because he was AJ)

Acknowledgements

Many people took part in the work on this book. Special thanks go to:

Jennifer Day
Holly Buchanan
Catherine McQuaid

To those who put up with questions and research,
To those who listened and debated,

And especially to those who got me out from behind the keyboard,

Boo and Ghost,

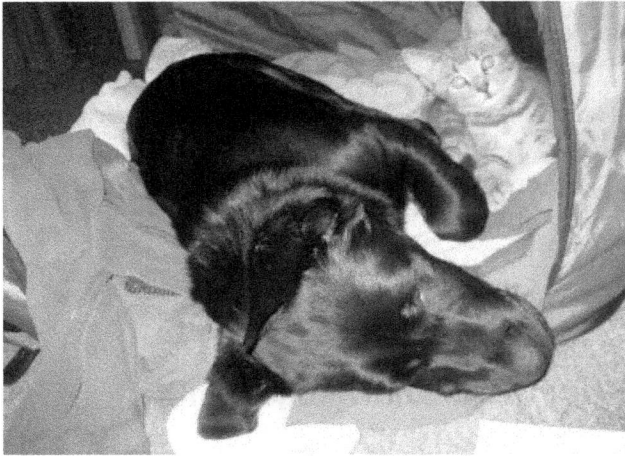

Thanks to you all.

Table of Contents

Take-Aways

Digital Resources for the Reading Virtual Minds *Series*

Some of the images in the *Reading Virtual Minds* series print editions are dark and difficult to read due to grayscaling and sizing issues. You can find high resolution, full color images of most charts and graphs used in this series at http://nlb.pub/rvm

Evolution Technology™ (ET), the technology described in this book and the external demonstration of much described in this series, is the foundation of several tools used for a variety of purposes by people ranging from lovers to politicians to businesspeople to researchers and more. You can watch a video explaining and using many of the tools developed from ET at http://nlb.pub/3

Please note that case matters ("A" isn't the same as "a") with all nlb.pub urls.

*Mankind never completely abandons
any of its ancient tools.
— Arthur C. Clarke*

About the Cover

My mother and I would go grocery shopping every Friday. She'd park under the elms across the street from Webster School (my gradeschool. They were once called "grammar" schools and are now called "elementary" schools, I think). There were morning and afternoon sessions with an hour in-between for lunch so students went home (students lived within a fifteen minute walk so going home wasn't a logistics challenge. Also, most families were dual parent, single income families so one parent was always home to take care of the children).

My mother realized that she could get me lunch, do her grocery shopping and get me back within the hour so it became a Friday ritual during my gradeschool years. She'd drive us to the Woolworth's lunch counter just across the parking lot from the Champaign's Supermarket on Valley Street in Manchester, New Hampshire.

I still remember the staff at the Woolworth's lunch counter. By name. Also their soft green uniforms with lace-edged, white half aprons, their bright white name patches with the red, script "Woolworth" and their equally red but unscripted names stitched in underneath, what they looked like, the sound of their voices, their scents, their smiles, their laughs, the feel of the light green Formica countertop, the dizzying feel as I'd spin on the red-topped, white trimmed lunch counter stool when I sat down, ...

I remember that elegantly tall, thin, chainsmoking Grace, her salt&pepper hair always pulled tightly into a bun or, if she'd just been to the hairdresser (a biweekly ritual) an enormous beehive, would always give me an extra scoop of coleslaw because I liked it so much, no charge, smiling at me with her tobacco stained teeth as she said in her gravely voice, "Here you go, hon," and that short, squat, pancaked make-uped Miriam – the Jeff to Grace's Mutt – who couldn't talk without a little laugh in her voice would save me the last piece of blueberry pie and if mother nodded there'd be a small scoop of creamily thick real vanilla ice-cream on top, and especially that mother wouldn't let me take a bite until I'd said my pleases and thankyous, then I was free to eat while she and the counter women caught up on the week's gossip.

This weekly ritual didn't take long. But the information exchanged between these three women – often augmented by petite, blond, full chested and dangerously young (that was how mother described her to dad, "dangerously young") Agnes who would call out comments from the grill which she never left except for once to give me a kiss when I graduated First Grade (she smelled deliciously of hamburgers) or heavily French accented Mauriça, the daughter of Quebec immigrants and who seemed to bathe in Avon™ Topaze™ and always walked proud and tall, her brunette hair always elegantly done, but who had to ask you to repeat yourself because she still translated everything you said into Quebeçois then back again before she answered you – then Mom and I would grocery shop and Mom would have me back before the 1 O'clock bell.

Take a moment and realize what the above indicates; There was a weekly, training ritual that taught me several social rituals necessary for survival:

    1 - Socializing. Think woodland animals teaching their
        young what other animals were safe, which weren't.
        Basically the learning of social skills.
    2 - Societalizing, of which "grocery shopping" is a piece.
        Think woodland animals teaching their young how to
        forage and hunt.

Now let's flash forward some fifty years to Facebook, LinkedIn, Twitter, FourSquare, Pinterest, Instagram, Vines, ones not yet known and others that may not survive. I'm sitting in an airport and hear two female voices giggling and cooing loudly but not to each other. It was a mother-daughter pair, the mother (I'm guessing) mid-thirties and the daughter (also guessing) late-single digits, both leaning with their backs against a window overlooking a jetway, both thin, both in designer jeans, both in ill-fitting, pink tank-tops, identical gold and precious stone bling in identical places, both with identical designer sunglasses pushed up into their identically blond highlighted, light brown hair, both with their arms crossed over their chests with one arm holding their identical cell phones to the same side ears heavy with the same huge gold hoop earrings, same rouged cheeks, red lipsticked lips and highlighted eyes showing amazement, distress, pouts and gleaming white teeth all the same way showing at the same words spoken the same way with the same emphasis at the same points in their conversations.[120]

How many times have you seen someone at a restaurant with their attention focused on a digital device and unaware of the people around them, the food before them or whatever's in the immediate vicinity that requires their attention? The building could be on fire and unless they receive a TXT about it, they're toast!

The lunch counter has become a computer screen, tablet or mobile device. Video is becoming more and more prevalent and won't be ubiquitous until transmission rates go down and pipes expand, and even then it's most likely the information will be primarily visual and auditory with some haptic (the vibratory "Manner Mode" on many mobile devices is an example) thrown in.[a] There's still a great deal of sensory information missing in today's online/digital social exchanges. If the daughter mentioned above ever meets any online friends in real life, we'll she be shocked that they're never buffered? Or will she wish they were so she could quietly sneak away while they were loading?

AC1 - Buffering, anyone?

Woolworth's messaging was clean and simple; Good food, things you need, fair prices. You wouldn't do your primary weekly shopping there, not even your speciality shopping (car parts, for example), but you'd always find those odd things you needed and

---

[a] – Nokia's Pavla Tomsová stated that data transmission eclipsed voice transmission in Dec 2010 at Ad:Tech San Francisco 2011. eMarketer stated that more people received their information on mobiles than on any other platform in mid 2011.443

get a cup of coffee, a slice of pie and good counter conversation with the staff and patrons to boot.

The mother and daughter pair mentioned above will never experience that. Nor, I think, would they want to. It would be the equivalent of dropping them into a strange and foreign land. People have no qualms about you hearing their personal and private phone conversations while you're shopping, but ask them about something in their basket and they have to pause a moment, perhaps internally buffering as they swipe their mental mobile phone interface off and load their in-person, talking interface on.

Woolworth's, in its day, knew how to attract the right people for the right reasons. I don't remember anybody walking out of a Woolworth's disappointed or empty handed[b]. Couldn't find exactly what you're looking for? Here's something else that'll do the job, costs the same, with some friendly salespeople to help you figure it out.

Need to think it over? Go try the pie. Tell them Grace sent you.

The desire to attract the right people and only for the correct reasons is especially true of virtual property[c] businesses wanting to attract consumers. Virtual properties are just another extension of our self-concept, of what we want others to believe about us,[78,122,151] another self-identification, another form of the creator (or creative team's collective) personality projected out into the world.[78]

And what's really meaningful in the transition of dominantly physical world social interactions to dominantly virtual world social interactions is the environmental information that is lost. Da Vinci's Vitruvian Man is surrounded by more immediately available information sources than ever before and the result?

People are spending so much time insulating themselves from information via unplugging and getting off the grid to the

---

[b] – I'm not counting the civil rights sit-in (see http://nlb.pub/10). Remember, these are the memories of young child in central New England.
[c] – digital, online, call them what you will. We use to call them "websites". So long as our biologic requirements are not immediately met by them, they do not exist in physical reality.

point that it's become a cultural catchphrase.[109] It shows up in commercials and as plot points in movies.[d]

But is it the variety of information sources people are escaping? Perhaps the lack of valued information?

Or perhaps people are discovering there's no real give and take. The information sources don't really care about the people as individuals – except as consumer data that can be sold to marketers – so why care about the information being provided?

I mean, do you really pay attention to everything that comes in on all your feeds? If you did, why would there be a market for autonomous agents such as GoogleNews that lets us specify what we want to know about?

And again the price is that Google sells those interests on.

Forget about Google's algorithms making decisions for us! We're no longer "browsing the stacks", an algorithm does that for us and we're the ones being browsed. That algorithm doesn't know us, our Core or even our Identity. It's just some programmer's best guess. How accurate can we expect it to be? People are more concerned that there's a digital slave market than that they're becoming digital slaves.

Where does it stop? Vitruvian Man's perfectly proportioned circle becomes a wide and fuzzy boundary.

I still have vivid memories of the Woolworth's counter ladies, still rich and full and sensorially real fifty-plus years later. I have no such environmental information of virtual world interactions so they are not as well anchored in memory. It's a good thing storage is increasingly inexpensive because the type of information provided by virtual properties and virtual personae are not designed to stay in memory long.[e]

---

[d] – From *Reading Virtual Minds Volume II: Experience and Expectation* (http://nlb.pub/RVMV21st):
The movie *While We're Young* has two couples from two different generations meeting and sharing, and it's the younger couple not wanting to use the 'net and stay offline. The phrase used is "We don't need to know. Let's just not know it. Let's not know what it is" and demonstrates a willingness to be satisfied with a lack of knowledge. This is a call to the mythic, to mystery, and away from digital, sensory reality. More myth, less fact. Still wanting to be involved, but in a way that is more satisfying to their Core than to their Personality.
[e] – Good thing people are increasingly relying on search engines to remember things for them, don't you think?303,403,552

Case in point, I couldn't identify an online "friend"'s projection (their chosen icon) into virtual reality. It was easier to recognize their projection when I was ignorant of its meaning than when I knew what it was.

AC2 - This is a chicken pecking. Once you know what it is, it's hard to see anything else. Until you know what it is, it's everything else.

What's meaningful is that my understanding, my awareness, my concept, my identification of my online friend is incredibly constrained by the medium, by my lack of first-person experience of them. The dance described in *Reading Virtual Minds Volume I: Science and History* is painfully restricted and most people don't know it's restricted, hence it becomes the norm and our understanding of those we interact with suffers.

The cover illustration demonstrates this restriction of our social awareness while building on some themes started if not stated in *Volume 1*:

1) The amount of information you can gather about an individual online is staggering.[70,98,99,141,351,363,449, 601,619]

2) It is staggeringly constrained by the medium used to gather that information...

3) ...unless you understand that each online decision semiotically points to two different things
   3.a) What aspects of their offline reality they want to share online and
   3.b) what aspects of their online reality they want to be identified by and with offline.[497]

4) And more than anything else, by the psycho-emotive, -cognitive and -behavioral landscape[31,67,69,70,80-82, 88,95,96,100,102,113,115,116,123,125-127,129-135,139-142,144,161,188, 189,219,242,288,290,313,359,375,382,398,436,445-447,454,463,470,490, 524,554,559,560] they've created for themselves that lies

between the borders they've placed around and
between their online and offline selves.

People are defined by the clothes they wear, the car they
drive, the devices they use and the choices they make. Especially
the choices they don't know that they're making. Especially the
choices they don't know that they're making when they're
communicating, online or off.

And it's much easier to project the "who" that we want to be
online than off because so much other information is missing in
online exchanges.

The Difference Between Women & Men

AC3 - If the only realities we share are our internal, online realities
we'll never be disappointed...but lo' to those who eventually wish to
meet reality-face to reality-face...

Sometimes our most misleading advertising is that which we
tell ourselves. People purchasing clothes online are pointing from
their online borderlands (the online stores they shop) to their
offline lives (the clothes they're purchasing[f]) with a great deal

---

[f] – Remember, there can be a difference between what is purchased and what is worn.
Fantasy life exists in the Core and Identity and rarely escapes to the Personality unless we
feel we are safe...like behind massive electron walls such as social networks like the early
AOL, Genie, CompuServe and more recently SecondLife use to provide.

more than the clothes purchased themselves. And you don't need NextStage's Evolution Technology to understand this. Something as simple as each item placed into a shopping cart, each item removed and if the cart is abandoned, are rich, vivid and meaning-laced statements of shoppers' lunch counter selves.

It's all there for the taking.

The amount of information you can gather about individuals without the use of personally identifying information (social security number, driver's license, login credentials, etc) is staggering. If you read *Reading Virtual Minds Volume I: Science and History* you know that it's possible to recognize individual A from individual B before they bounce (online and it doesn't matter what device – smartphone, PDA, iPad, tablet, iPhone, 3G, 4G, ... – they're using) and how it can be done.

The down side of this is something psychologically healthy children sitting at lunch counters never experience; Paranoia[g]. Activists are concerned about the safety of our personally identifying information but the truth is that the majority of people in modern societies gave up their privacy and individuality by the time they started school and definitely by the time they graduated college.[22,89,145,162,169,245,250,318,327,351,417,458,544,575,578,598]

After all, how many people do you see commuting to work on a unicycle?

And those who are commuting on a unicycle? They're using streets and sidewalks, right? They're not going from rooftop to rooftop. When I started the *Reading Virtual Minds* series back in 2003 the *SegWay* was a joke. Now not so much so.

Remember readers, the history of technology is the study of placing the most power into the greatest number of human hands economically.[87,124,128,130,137,143]

The up side of this is that our communications channels – mobiles, tablets, smartphones, computers, netbooks, cable, satellite and radio presets, what we load onto our mpg players and iPods™ – are one of the last bastions of our individualities.

---

[g] – The best definition of paranoia I've ever encountered, "Paranoia is the inability to understand why there *wouldn't* be someone waiting for you behind the tree."[145]

Or at least they were until we started sharing our playlists, address books, etc., on social sites.

We work at making our Facebook, Naymz, LinkedIn, Pandora, Amazon, eBay, Twitter, Xing, ReferralKey and other profiles, our desktops, palmtops, avatars and so on as unique as we can via background images, icons, color choice, ...

And again, if you read *Reading Virtual Minds Volume I: Science and History*[h] you know that all those choices you made in order to assert your individuality broadcast more than you could hope to imagine, identify you in ways you could never have dreamed, reveal secrets of your love life, your childhood, your worklife, your fears, hopes and dreams in ways both beautiful and terrifying.

The choices you made to show how individual you are do much more than uniquely identify and brand you, they also reveal how you think, how you make decisions, what happened in your life, what was important to you to you when you made those decisions, what's important to you now when you make new decisions, ...

When you change them, you're demonstrating that some part of you has changed, has grown, has become something new and different, something that was not has become some one that is.

Know what was, know who is, and you can predict with amazing accuracy when the next change will come, what it will be, how long things will last as they are before changes occur, ...

Know who you are now and for how long you've been this version of "you" and predicting what new you will come next and when is child's play.[i]

---

[h] – http://nlb.pub/RVMV14th

[i] – I know you'll be shocked when I tell you there's an equation for this. The average person doesn't need the equation, though, only some good common sense and the ability to self-observe. Think of a double pan balance. In one pan is everything that you're contented with, the other pan is everything you're discontented with. Note, *contented* and *discontented*. not happy or unhappy. We're talking mild emotional load, not major emotional load. When more things from the contented pan to the discontented pan than move from the discontented to contented, a behavioral and/or *identity change is in the offing, perhaps even a Core change*. Note also, it's not the total emotional load in each pan, it's the number of elements in each pan.

Now for the really scary part. You're not really making the decisions any more regarding what you broadcast into the world. You're making selections from an interface that someone else designed according to some other group's concept of greatest usability. People create unique identities from pre-defined elements and if they're predefined, they're not truly unique. Not even some wild combination of them.

Because the truly unique within a defined system causes that system to break. Societies, like machines, work best when everything is well defined and kept tightly in place. Add something unique to a machine or a society and, if that unique element survives, the society and machine fail.

Marshall McLuhan[j] wrote that the medium was the message. That is still true with one slight difference. The difference comes from my "The history of technology is placing power in the most people's hands economically" axiom.

The medium is still the message. The difference is that we're becoming the medium. And if we (as individuals) are becoming the medium, what is our message (collectively and individually)?

Our communication technologies are placing more and more social power into our hands more and more economically. Years ago if we saw someone walking down the street talking to nobody we assumed they were upset, homeless, crazy...definitely nothing positive. Now we assume they're BlueToothing or singing along with whatever's coming through their earbuds. And most importantly, those earbudding are paying attention to neither an external nor internal reality. Am I describing you during your commute? Then you're unaware of your environment and yourself in it.[k]

---

[j] – Http://en.wikipedia.org/wiki/Marshall_McLuhan
[k] – This may seem like simple multi-tasking to you and remember, from *Reading Virtual Minds Volume II: Experience and Expectation*, that people can't multi-task:
People may think they can multitask and they can't, at least not in a way that leads to multiple task productivity unless the individual tasks are so minor that no task-directed cognitive effort is required to perform them.164,171,272,303,354,416,435,507,580 What humans are remarkably good at is *serial tasking*. We may have several things going on around us and we're taking part in all of them but only one at a time.

Much as our ancestors gave up the freedom of the pampas for the security of the city – the constraints of "as far as the eye could see" becoming laws, mores and physical walls – many are giving up the security of direct personal contact for the freedom of the internet – where the laws, mores and walls are highly in flux.

So the medium is still the message.

And from *Reading Virtual Minds Volume I: Science and History*, you are the medium.

The medium to what? The *go-between* from what to what?

Ah, well...from the world to your mind and back.

But if the world in your mind has no basis in the world in which you're physical needs are met? I have one word for students entering college in the early 21st century.

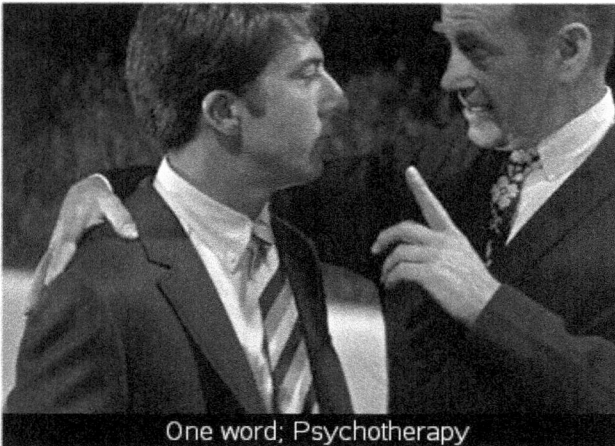

One word; Psychotherapy

A9 - If Walter Brooke's Mr. McGuire were counseling Dustin Hoffman's Graduate today, the word would be "psychotherapy".

Want to be an individual? That means controlling your own message. That takes effort, though, an effort most people aren't willing to make in our increasingly networked world. Few people can look into the face of God and live, fewer people understand that the first god they must please is the one facing them in the mirror and the fewest people are willing to look into the mirror, see and understand what is revealed about themselves in that god's face.[146]

That reflection in your computer or mobile screen? Is that you or who you want people to see? The greater the difference the less you'll be able to control your own message.

Foreword
by Susan Carrabis

I've wanted the *Fair-Exchange* chapter (that's right, all of this book was one chapter in the original book Joseph wrote) in the *Reading Virtual Minds* books since the beginning, but the material didn't fit into Volume I or II. At last my wait is over! It's here in Volume III. Now you can have as much fun with it as I do. People who know me call Fair-Exchange "Susan's Big Hammer" and now you'll find out why.

The concept of Fair-Exchange answers many questions I've had over the years. Before I was introduced to Fair-Exchange I always wondered why a movie left me unsatisfied, why a book left me wanting more, why going someplace or being with someone sometimes left me feeling unsatisfied. I had a good time, didn't I?

So why was I unhappy? The answer was, as I came to learn, that there was no *fair-exchange* between me and whatever I was doing at the time. Most people would say "I felt that I was giving way more than I was getting out of a situation" and they're on the right track but going in the wrong direction.

People give of themselves, their property, their time all the time and don't think of some kind of reward for their efforts. But some reward does exist even if they don't know what it is, and it's the "getting" of that reward that makes the giving possible.

It's not "giving more than you get", it's "not getting equal to what you give". Read those again. The differences are subtle and more profound than you think. Or were for me, at least.

Becoming aware of Fair-Exchange changed the way I do things. It really changed my life in little and large ways; I'm an avid reader and usually have 2-3 books going at the same time. I always felt that once I started a book I always had to finish it. Not sure why, but I did. It was even worse than that! I couldn't start a new book until I'd finished the one I was reading. It was AGONY!

After incorporating this concept into my life I no longer have to finish a book that's not engaging me. Now with this new tool in my consciousness, I give a book so many pages and if I don't care if the characters live or die, I'm on to another book. I now understand that I was getting nothing from the book, no enjoyment at all, although I was giving of myself, my time which is precious, and the exchange between me and the book wasn't fair at all.

Readers with a psychodynamics background know that the "give more than you get" is a victimizing mentality, and altruism and self-victimizing behavior can become cozy bedfellows if you're not watching. Lots of businesses, governments, non-profits and related organizations encourage their clients, citizens, members and participants to walk this altruism to self-victimizing corridor as often as possible. People feel they can't break away from a company that's treating them poorly, can't switch brands, move to another location or stop taking part because *giving* is something we're taught is a social good since childhood.

Fair-Exchange's "get as good as you give" frees people from walking that corridor. They can still walk it, but now they understand that they're doing it and that it's their choice, not their obligation, and they now have the power to recognize their choice as part of the fair-exchange calculation.

Hopefully this book and the Fair-Exchange concept will open your eyes as it did mine and change your perception of things. Knowledge is a good thing and when you understand why you feel the way you do about something then you are empowered to change it. I still do things where I know it's not quite a Fair-Exchange, but knowing this beforehand I have the power to make sure that the exchange is a little more fair then it used to be. I also give myself permission to not do things because I know going in that I don't want to be involved in something where there's no hope of a Fair-Exchange happening.

Have you ever gone to the movies, stayed 'til the end and then said "That's two hours of my life I'll never get back?'" Now-a-days it's more like three hours and let's not forget the cost! This is another example of no Fair-Exchange. We gave our time and the movie failed to do its part; it didn't entertain us for that same period of time. We now choose to watch movies at home. That way we can do other things and best of all we can turn it off and do something else if we don't like the movie or are tired of dropped signals and buffering!

TV shows, with all the commercials, weren't holding my attention either. The shows were poorly written, got predictable, name your reason. There was no Fair-Exchange with all of the commercial interruptions. I started reading books during the commercials and suddenly realized that the show I'd been watching had ended and I never noticed because I was still reading. My book gave a better Fair-Exchange then the show did.

Anybody remember "Tivo-Guilt", "Voluntary Simplification", "Email Bankruptcy" and things like that? All are examples of Fair-Exchange, both good and bad, and now we have the knowledge and power to control the Exchange!

In general don't waste your time on things that aren't a Fair-Exchange unless you are prepared ahead of time. There may be times when you give more than you get but overall there needs to be a balance. An author may disappoint me once and I'll try another of their books, but keep disappointing me and I'm finding someone new to read.

Likewise, an exchange may be best for the other person now, and the exchange becomes fair later because that's when your "get" is as good as your "give". If you've ever heard of "karma-feedback" then you know what this is. Somebody recently tweeted the message in figure SF1 on page 32.

It's a great demonstration of how fair-exchange wins in the end. The tweeter rejoiced because, in the end, they got as good as they gave, meaning fair-exchange works on more levels than consciousness and economics, it involves emotional, physical, spiritual and psychological dynamics.

We can't always be on the giving end of things. Whether it's our time, money, expertise or whatever. If we don't get at least as good as we give then the relationship created with a person, product, book, TV show, company won't last. If you're constantly giving and not getting – the Altruism to Self-Victimization

Corridor – it causes resentment and this leads to an end of the relationship. Either with a person, company, product, book...you name it.

I Love Karma

Sean Sparling
@sasagronomy

The man who just drove into the parking space I was waiting for & told me to F off, has arrived for his interview - WITH ME! #karmawinsagain

SF1 - Karma is best served cold

And what we get in return doesn't have to be what we give. We could give our time and get money in return or an emotional lift by helping someone. We decide what the exchange is and we decide if it's fair. It doesn't matter if someone else thinks it's a Fair-Exchange. It's what we think that matters.

And oh yea! There's lots of other stuff in this book that you'll get a lot out of. I really love the Fair-Exchange part.

Kind a noticed that from this intro, did ya?

What monstrosities would walk the streets were some people's faces as unfinished as their minds.

- Eric Hoffer

Author's Foreword

Hello.

It's me again, Joseph, the author.

This book, like *Reading Virtual Minds Volume II: Experience and Expectation*[a] before it, was a section in the original *Reading Virtual Minds Volume I: Science and History*. Amazing, isn't it, what I had packed in that original volume? Glad we broke it all out? Well, you should be!

What amazes me more than anything else is how little updating's been required since the mid 2000s when I wrote that original tome. Sure, some things have changed but the brain hasn't. The mechanics of how we interact socially has changed but how we internalize those social interactions hasn't.

We're still us regardless of the devices used.

I've written in many places that whatever's inside of us eventually gets outside of us:

> What's so fascinating about this is that [teaching]'s also how we pass on our core, personality and identity beliefs whether we mean to or not (I cover this in detail in Reading Virtual Minds Volume I: Science and History). We can be teaching physics, soccer, piano, bread-baking, ... It doesn't matter because all these activities will be vectors for our core, identity and personal beliefs and behaviors. If we are joyful people then we will teach others to be joyful and the vector for that lesson will be physics, soccer, piano, bread-baking, ... And if we are miserable people? Then we will teach others to be miserable and to be so especially when they do physics, play soccer, the piano, bake bread, ...
>
> Thus if any teaching/training occurs intentionally or otherwise, the individual doing the training/teaching is going to de facto teach their internal philosophies and beliefs — both business and personal — as well as their methods and practices to their students. This can't be helped. It's how humans function. ...[149]

Let me share some real life examples of this.

---

[a] – You can get copies of all my books on Amazon at http://nlb.pub/jdcamazon

I was walking with a friend through Boston on a comfortably warm Spring day. Downtown Boston was its usual bustle of pedestrians and vehicular traffic and we joined right in. We'd started walking around 10am, hadn't stopped, just talking as we walked up and down parts of the BackBay and it was now a little after noon.

My friend suggested we get lunch.

"Good idea. Let's."

At which point he pulled out his iPhone, started the camera and began scanning images of the street we were on, the apartment buildings, the shops, ...

"What are you doing?"

He had an app that could recognize where we were by the images captured then tell you what's in the area.

"Really?"

Neat, huh?

I shook my head. "Watch carefully." I turned to someone walking past us. "Excuse me, sir, we're visitors here. Could you recommend a good restaurant for lunch? Nothing fancy. A sandwich shop is fine."

And we got a wonderful description of where to go for what, several options presented, suggestions for what to do after lunch, a genuine conversation, a give and take, an exchange, thankyous, you'rewelcomes, smiles and handshakes.

My friend was dumbfounded.

I. Am. Not. Kidding.

He actually said it never occurred to him to just ask someone. After all, he had that app.

That failed.

The takeaway is that his device had more reality to him than the hundreds of people walking around him.

I'm glad he's not running for president. I don't want his finger anywhere near a button that can do more than launch an app that separates him from interacting with his species.

Or perhaps I'm incorrect regarding his species.

Budda-boom.

Another time I'd made an appointment to Skype with someone. They missed the appointment. So it goes, such things happen. We rescheduled. They missed that appointment, too, and offered "I'm officially too unreliable to schedule and make a meeting..." along with the suggestion that I schedule through his assistant.

But they asked for and scheduled the meeting, not me, both times.

What was his assistant going to do? Chain him to a phone at the time of the call?

No, his assistant was going to make sure the appointment made it into his scheduling...app.

I guess in a world where person-to-person interactions are disappearing personal responsibility disappears as well (see *Chapter 6 – Fair-Exchange, Privacy, Identity and Digital Divisivity*, page 98).

These experiences and similar others led to NextStage Principle #70:

> *Technology is not how we make and keep relationships. We make and keep relationships because of who we are, not what tools we use to stay in touch.*
> Everybody's lives are hectic. If you can't get everything done you want to do and are missing appointments/meetings/friends/what-have-you, getting more technology won't organize your day because time isn't your problem, you are. You have as much time in your day as Michelangelo, Galileo, Newton, Einstein, Gandhi, Mother Teresa, Buddha, Socrates, ... [b]

Lastly, someone was having a personal challenge and I shared my home phone number with the instructions "Please do not share this with anyone. It is our private number and we want to keep it that way."

You know where this is going, I'm sure. This individual not only shared our home number, they cced me on the email in which they shared our private number and wrote "This is Joseph's

[b] – http://www.nextstagevolution.com/principles.cfm#70

private home phone number which he expressly requested I not share."

Forgive my incredulity and *HUH?*

In the first example above, *Fair-Exchange* didn't exist between the individual and the people around him therefore he could not establish a social network with them.

Unless they could be accessed through a device.

Sad, don't you think?

In the second example, what I value isn't what the other person values so *Fair-Exchange* can not exist between us and communication fails.

The third example is another example of unshared values and again, communication fails. The difference between the second and third examples is object value versus concept value. The former is time,[138,232,435,442,459] the latter is privacy.[5,89,145,282,294, 327,427,480,598] The former is difficult to recoup, the latter is increasingly difficult to achieve and in both cases, the exchange was not fair so both parties either lose out on further negotiations or employ a third party to negotiate for them (see Chapter 2 – Negotiating a Fair-Exchange, page 58, for more on this).

This book is all about *Fair-Exchange*, the giving and getting that must take place internally before any giving and getting can successfully take place externally, and how social networks rely on it without knowing its name.

And in keeping with that Fair-Exchange concept, this book is much easier to understand if you've read Volumes I and II, and in that order. Fair warning to help conduct a fair-exchange.

And in case you didn't notice, I still use personal examples. Much easier to keep track that way.

Enjoy.

1 – Fair-Exchange, or "You Have to Give As Good As You Get"

What is a "fair-exchange"? In tribal societies and according to pop culture, it's when two people give each other something and both walk away happy. In other words, it's a "good trade". Anthro- and paleo-economists would argue that fair-exchange evolved as follows:

> "I'll give you this if you give me that" haggling led to "the principle of parity exchange"[504] which in turn led to barter which led to
> both fair-exchange[35,46,534,591,623] and the "Golden Rule,"[19,39,49,235,238,252,260,325,434,585a]
>
> then evolved into modern commerce systems (currency in all its forms)[235,238,260,504,585]

and those last two items, the "fair-exchange to modern information commerce" offers an important Take-Away for device designers:

Take-Away #1 – When product size no longer determines value then value is measured by ability/capability. The willingness to pay premiums for smaller personal devices is based on those devices performing more and more desired functions

---

[a] – Lots of research has been done on "the generosity of the internet" and it's sad to think that not long ago it was used as an example of large scale generosity: "For those who question the viability of large scale generous behavior, think no further than the Internet, the most extraordinarily open and generous artifact. The Internet is generous in two ways. Firstly, in the ethos of freely giving and sharing which stubbornly persists in the face of all attempts to commercialize. And secondly, in the actual hardware structure of the Internet. Anarchy can work! See John Naughton's (1999) wise and wide-ranging discussion of computing and the Internet and Tim Berners-Lee (1999), the creator of the World Wide Web, for his account of sustaining and managing generosity. " (from *Does large scale generosity work? The internet as a {modern/information} cornucopaeia*)

Tom Connor[b], a consulting economist whose opinions and values I trust, told me that economics has the idea of "fair market value" and I'm sure it grew out of the anthropologic fair-exchange model. Tom and others[c] define fair market value as follows:

> The price that an interested but not desperate buyer would be willing to pay and an interested but not desperate seller would be willing to accept on the open market assuming a reasonable period of time for an agreement to arise.

I'll accept the above as a definition for how a market determines a value on a good or service if one element is added regarding "open market"; The open market which sets the fair market value is an arbitrarily large but indeterminate group and usually evolves over time[d]. If enough people are willing to pay x for item z, then the fair market value of z is x. The above – with or without modification – isn't a definition of a fair-exchange. For one thing, most people have an innate – albeit sometimes erroneous – concept of what constitutes a fair-exchange. If you've ever heard someone say "Do you know how long I had to work to afford that?" you're hearing a statement of fair-exchange, not of fair market value. Likewise, when most people are researching the purchase of a non-staple item (a car, for example) they might decide that the item isn't worth the asking price even if the market sustains that price. Again, you're witnessing fair-exchange, not fair market value. A fellow I know started his software development business by going to potential clients and saying "Let me work for you for a month for no charge. If you don't like what I'm doing, we part company no questions asked, if you like my work you pay me for my time and I get a contract." To this fellow, what was fair was the chance to prove himself over a given time in exchange for guaranteed long-term relationships.

---

[b] – http://tomconnor.hungrypeasant.com
[c] – http://www.investorwords.com/1880/fair_value.html
[d] – My studies cause me to conclude that evolutionary forces shape the world and economics (with energy as the currency) drive evolutionary forces.

There is another example of fair-exchange which is known by every US schoolchild (maybe. Who knows what they're teaching these days?) – the Colonists buying the island of Manhattan for a few glass beads. Would anybody care to argue the trade was for fair market value, even in its day?

But, if it really happened at all, it was an example of a fair-exchange. Let me give you a whimsical take on the post trade conversations. First, the Amerinds:

> "Hey, Nunpa, where'd you get those bright shiny things?"
> "You're not going to believe this. I met a bunch of yahoos who wanted to know if I owned Turtle Island!"[e]
> Much laughter, then, "What's 'owned'?"
> "I don't know, but they pointed to the ground then swept their arms around and looked all around them toward the horizon then asked if I wanted to trade these bright shiny things for everything they could see. What a bunch of yucks!"
> "My God! Are they still around? Think they'll want to trade for Great Sky Lake[f]?"

Our Amerind friends are laughing so hard they need to hold each other up otherwise they'd fall to the ground.

> "I know! Who'd'a thunk it? They had a whole bag of these and didn't put a-one on their clothes. It's as if they didn't know bright shiny beads are signs of power! And what did they want in exchange? Something everybody can see and goes on forever! And they didn't even care about the best fishing spots! And the beavers are way up over there! They didn't even know enough to ask! What nin-cow-poops! What maroons!"

And our two Amerinds walk off holding the bright shiny beads up to the sun, talked about the pretty colors and such, and thinking themselves wise and grand.

---

[e] – "Turtle Island" is a supposed Amerind name for the entire North American continent, "Great Sky Lake" for the Atlantic Ocean.
[f] – If humans evolves from fish and not apes, there'd be no interest in land property. But the price of a deep sea trough would be mohorovicic!

Meanwhile, back at the Colonists' camp...

> "Harold, you old dog! I thought I'd wet myself when you showed those ignorant savages those glass beads. Who's the man? Who's the man?"
> "Yeah, I know. I almost felt bad about it, but they didn't seem to mind. It's the price of ignorance, you know."
> "And look at the navigation channels! The harbors! They didn't know what they had. What are you going to call it? Haroldville? No, let's do what those Italians did and use the family name. What did they call it? Vespucciland? I'm going for Meinplatzenalles. And we can put in some golf courses right over there, see? ..."
> Mutual laughter and backslapping.
> "I was going to ask them to throw in the Atlantic for another bead but figured nobody could be that dumb."
> "Oh, you should've gone for it. You should've gone for it."

This is funny (I hope) due to a clash of cultures and beliefs. Amerinds had no concept of land ownership because there was no psychological or economic need for such. Their cultural development was based on completely different concepts and metaphors than those used by the colonists. They understood *use* and not *ownership*, and if something was *useful* then anybody with a need could use that thing until the current user no longer had the need or someone else had a greater need.

Europeans, however, had very firm and fixed concepts of property and ownership. The concept of *use* was subsumed by *ownership* as in "only the person who owned a thing could use it or decide who could use it." The idea that a resource shouldn't be psychologically and economically exploited was as beyond their understanding as was land ownership to the Amerinds.

But the real key to understanding beads-for-Manhattan is that a fair-exchange took place. The Amerinds valued the land as a spiritual metaphor; it was endless therefore couldn't be depleted therefore couldn't be owned. Denying someone rights to the land was equivalent to the Colonists denying someone the right of Baptism. The land had no economic value to the Amerinds, therefore trading it for a few shiny objects never before seen that let others know how powerful you were? I mean, everybody (at least other Amerinds) knew that bright shiny objects that had never been seen before were demonstrations of power, right?

Well, if those funny talking people on the big canoe wanted to...

The Colonists also had something of little economic value; glass beads.

Ah, but in the cultural paradigms of the other? Shiny objects never before seen that indicated power? That was great value. And to the Colonists? Land as far as the eye could see with natural harbors and excellent deep water navigation? That was great value.

Fair-exchange, you begin to understand, occurs first in the heart and in the mind only after the fact. It has very little to do with the purse and wallet. People who believe they have been swindled believe so because what they thought was a fair-exchange wasn't. Someone may rob from you or steal from you and you've lost some possessions. Ah, but if someone swindles you? That is a personal violation and must be met with the harshest penalties regardless of the law. Personal violations, remember, are injuries to our identity and often to our core. A swindler has caused you to question your belief in yourself and such people, those who force us to look into the face of our inner gods and demons, must be damned.[g]

The traditional "you have to give as good as you get" is turned around; you have to get as good as you give. In interhuman interactions, be they combat or grocery shopping or fly-fishing with some friends, we determine our own and the "other"'s worth by "how well they take a punch", "how well they take a joke" and so on, meaning the person who repeatedly offends but is intolerant of being offended is cast aside eventually if not immediately.[h] The person who gives of themselves but

---

[g] – Think Bernie Madoff and you get the idea.
[h] – If you fall into this camp, make sure you're always valuable to those around you. The moment your value becomes less than your maintenance, the fair-exchange fails and you're denied your social heaven

takes nothing in return becomes a caricature open to socio-economic abuse, the person who laughs at others but can't tolerate being laughed at themself is the person mocked and derided.

In all these things, you have to get as good as you give or the social exchange stops. The concept of fair-exchange engages whenever there is a "give-and-get" (Note: not a "give-and-take") occurring and is so closely tied to experience and expectations[i] that to ignore its existence is to lose opportunities. To deny its importance is to offer what's not wanted and to expect what you'll never get. Information designers, usability and experience designers, marketers, negotiators, ... need to understand how specific aspects of exchange play into the minds of people interacting with information on digital properties, billboards, presentations, webinars, brochures, kiosks, each other, et cetera, and how these aspects affect their expectations and experience. When the negotiator is a human agent, both parties need to trust that that human agent has their best interests at heart. That same trust, in the virtual world, gets transferred to the interface and often with uncomfortable and unfortunate consequences.

The balance that allows fair-exchange is a multidimensional one (figure 1.1, page 44). Fair-exchange is always between two or more people and the exchange emotionally, physically, spiritually and psychologically rich and complex. It is not a balance of "what I give equals what I get", which is fair value and the individual giving and getting decides if any exchange will take place. Going back to our cultural clash metaphor, fair value is along a well recognized, Western educational and cultural axis; physical-psychological. This *physical* thing has that *psychological* value. This would be a wonderful working criteria if we were all linear-logical creatures and we're not despite what five-thousand years of Hellenic training has instilled in us. We are complex creatures and even the multi-dimensionality of the fair-exchange matrix (figure 1.1, page 44) is simplified greatly.

---

[i] – Covered in detail in *Reading Virtual Minds Volume II: Experience and Expectation*,

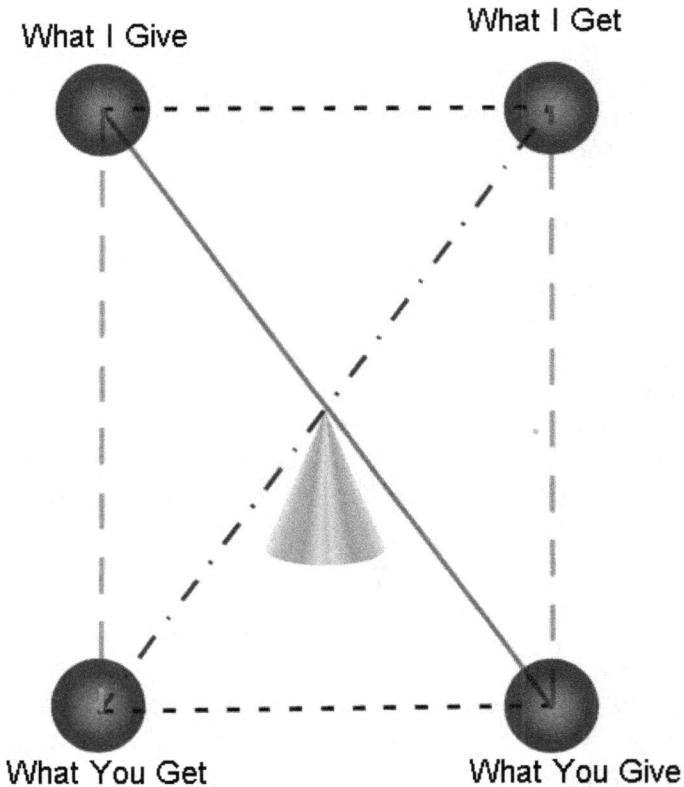

1.1 - All Fair-Exchanges are multidimensional in nature

Fair-exchange comes down to this: What I give must balance with what you give, what I get must balance with what you get. Fair-exchange deals with concepts of emotional, physical, spiritual and psychological value, it has nothing to do with "this thing at this price" value concepts.[175] The "sides" of the scale

=====

(representing different dimensions or axes) must balance (and this is where thinking multidimensional works to one's benefit):

- If I believe that what I'm giving you is worthless then you must also believe that what you're giving me is worthless. It doesn't matter if I think what you're giving me are the keys to the kingdom, all that matters is that the value you assign to what you're giving me equals the value I assign to what I'm giving you. This is represented by the red (solid line) axis going from upper left to lower right, "What I Give" to "What You Give"
- If I believe that what I'm getting from you are the keys to the kingdom then you must also believe that what you're getting from me are the keys to the kingdom, if I believe that what I'm getting from you is worthless then you must also believe what you're getting from me is worthless. This is represented by the blue (dash dot dash line) axis from lower left to upper right, "What You Get" to "What I Get"
- My emotional state regarding what I give and what you get must equal your emotional state regarding what you give and what I get. This is represented by the left and right top to bottom green (long dash) lines, the "What I Give - What You Get" side must balance with "What I Get - What You Give" side
- My psychological state regarding what I give and what I get must be equal to your psychological state regarding what you give and what you get. If I think I'm getting the better of you then you must think you're getting the better of me, if I think I'm getting taken then you must think you're getting taken. The bottom black (short dash) "What You Get - What You Give" side must balance with top black (short dash) "What I Get - What I Give" side

The red (solid) line must be in balance, the blue (dash dot dash) line must be in balance, the greens (long dash) must balance and the blacks (short dash) must balance. Imbalance any of these axes and the exchange will fail, either immediately or down the road and here's where we up the ante; immediate failures can be rectified to everyone's satisfaction. Immediate failures are usually simple miscommunications during negotiations and not intentional attempts to swindle, rob, cheat or steal.

But failures down the road? Failures down the road become non-returning customers, debranded customers, antagonistic customers, dissatisfied customers, buyers remorse and regret and these are just the beginnings.

Let's use our Colonists and Amerinds to demonstrate this:

- The Amerinds gave something to which they assigned no value and the Colonists gave something to which they assigned no value. Red (solid line) axis balance!
- The Amerinds received something to which they assigned high value and the Colonists received something to which they assigned high value. Blue (dash dot dash) axis balance!
- The Amerinds thought they were hustling the Colonists and the Colonists thought they were hustling the Amerinds. Green (long dash) axes balance!
- The Amerinds thought they were getting a lot for a little and the Colonists thought they were getting a lot for a little. Black (short dash) axes balance!

What the Amerinds gave balanced with what the Colonists got - nothing of value - at least as far as the Amerinds were concerned, and vice versa. Contrast this with a fair value; Something was marked at US$40 and you paid US$40 for it. You're either happy with your purchase or not and you're the only one you need to please. The "market" set the value and you accepted it or not. If you didn't accept the market price someone else in the market would, so the market, that arbitrarily big and largely anonymous group, didn't care.

The Amerinds got something they valued highly and the Colonists got something they valued highly. The Colonists gave up something they didn't value and so did the Amerinds, and so it goes for the rest. If either side's emotional meters differed from that belief the exchange would never have taken place.

What's interesting about the concept of fair-exchange and a good trade is that we're still a tribal society, we just have different elements to indicate which tribe we're in. Just as the Maori and other societies perform ritual tattooing, so do we. Remember the "power tie"? How about the "business suit"? Ted Williams never wore a suit and he was both respected and hated because of it, depending which side of the table you sat on in relation to him. No less a personality than Walter Cronkite recognized the power of tribal identity in his autobiographical *A Reporter's Life*[j]:

> It is always easier for an affluent society such as ours, and particularly one linked by heritage and relationship to the cultivated societies of Europe, to side with a regime that seeks to duplicate and preserve the looks and demeanor of our lifestyle, to which we are accustomed, rather than to embrace those whose native culture and appearance are different from our own.

In one short paragraph the most trusted man in America explains why some people will succeed in business with no more asset than personality and others with assets of time, energy and knowledge will fail, why some will be trusted and others despised and all for no greater a reason than that the former looked the part, knew the words and could play the role others required of them.[k] A fair-exchange took place even though no physical goods were involved. Remember this the next time you vote.

---

[j] – http://nlb.pub/X
[k] – As a co-worker recently shared, "I think being good at something is not necessarily the key prerequisite to being successful at something."

Where does fair-exchange come from? Like everything else we've talked about so far, it comes from childhood. Specifically, from what's called *social play behavior* and quite specifically from our primary care-givers during those first months of life.[29,30,273,335,348,618] Clinicians use the term *socially retarded* for children raised without fair-exchanging primary care-givers (Romanian orphanages under Ceausescu demonstrated this beyond all doubt). Social play behavior's roots are in *shared social problem solving*. Both are critical for healthy brain development[273] and this is an important element for information designers, UXers, property and content developers, et cetera.

Take-Away #2 – The more you get your audience/visitors/users to be proactive and reafferent with your interface/tool/product/site the more positively engaged and branded they will be

Take-Away #3 – The more your audience/visitors/users believe you're working with them to help them achieve their goal the more positively engaged and branded they will be

Social play behavior isn't restricted to humans and much of the research in these lines has been done in animal ethology. Like humans, animals have expectations, "concepts" if you will, of how any communication should turn out. Are expectations unmet? Then the animal (or human) believes it has been treated unfairly.[27,46,52,238,263,277,281,304,307,315,346,399,586,614]

How does the animal or human know what kind of behavior to expect (and by extension, when it has been treated unfairly)? By learning to recognize certain *markers* in the communication (and once again semiotics rears its head). These markers indicate different interests between individuals involved in the communication. Markers such as "I want to rest" and "I want to work" are rampant in western society and many people have felt themselves under the gaze of a boss' hairy eyeball more than once because they wanted to rest and the boss wanted them to work. Other markers include "I want to rest" and "I want to play" between spouses (and much marital discord occurs when these markers are unrecognized or ignored), "I want attention" and "I want to be left alone" between friends or co-workers, and others.

Have you ever yelled at, directed foul language at, threw down, tossed aside, kicked, spoken unkindly towards or otherwise directed negative energy at some appliance, tool, device or interface that failed to perform as desired or advertised?

Congratulations, you were experiencing and demonstrating a failed fair-exchange between yourself and whatever it was, this time along the usable - experience, usability - expectation fair-exchange axes. You're assigning a value to something, perhaps your time and/or effort, and the whatever isn't assigning equal value to its contribution. Perhaps it's not living up to marketing hype, perhaps it's not as easy to use as you were led to believe, perhaps it's not worth the money you spent, perhaps you haven't read the directions carefully or correctly. Remember that humans create community with whatever's around them?[90] Welcome to a failed community created by failed marketing and failed collateral. *Ooftah!*

What's interesting from the *Reading Virtual Minds* point of view is that what's subtly going on when markers are exchanged is a negotiation, a give-and-get, and the consequences of misuse of these markers are extreme because the marker is believed before the word or deed is. Misuse of markers can result in the simple "I'm getting mixed signals here" or can lead to life altering events such as divorce or ostracism[i]. Let me give you an example of something in between the two, something recognized as the mixed signal dichotomies of the venture capitalist telling the farmer "I think I can help you" – a mutually familiar phrase with completely different meanings for the two cultures leaving both shocked when a fair-exchange doesn't occur.

---

[i] – As an interesting point, ostracism is how children conceive of death – being alone.

An investor contacted me because of our Principles page[m]. He said, "Anybody willing to put that up on a website is somebody I want to meet." The majority of conversations we had were life-based, not work-based. This investor grew up on a farm and worked as a laborer in his early years. I spent my early years on dairy farms, driving trucks and working in warehouses. When I asked the investor to tell me about himself, he started with amusing anecdotes from childhood, shared successes and failures, important moments and tender moments.

Contrast this with the investor who, when asked to tell me about himself physically pulled back and responded with "I don't want this to be about class." I was so unprepared for that response I wasn't sure I'd heard him correctly. Upon requestioning him I realized I had correctly understood his response; he viewed me as something emotionally, psychologically, spiritually and possibly physically foreign, alien, and most definitely unlike him in so many ways that he could easily separate the two of us into distinct and different classes. ET's parsing of that statement produces the non-conscious communication "I make you different from me."[74] The speaker, for whatever reason, needed to believe he was unlike me. *Ouch.*

The earlier mentioned investor and two other successful gentlemen understood my "I need some help" signals as I understood them. These three grew up on farms and worked in blue-collar jobs. The three of them shared experiences and language and were able to exchange signals with me that made me feel comfortable with them. Anyone who is idiomatically multi-lingual understands what was happening in this anecdote. These three gentlemen were multi-signual and – just as someone idiomatically multi-lingual shifts identities depending on the language they're speaking (not Personalities, just the identities manifesting those personalities) – were able to act as agents, mentors, guides, et cetera, to bring me into the world of business and investing. One identity manifested to explain things to me in terms and with signals and signs I would accept and understand.

---

[m] – http://nlb.pub/J

Another identity manifested when discussing ET to the business world.

What is worth remembering from this anecdote is that butchers can learn business from butchers more readily than they can from bakers or candlestick makers and vice versa. The other item of note is that if the butchers, the bakers and candlestick makers think you're insane, get yourself checked into an asylum before you hurt somebody. But if the butchers and bakers think you're okay and only the candlestick makers think you're insane, the problem is with the candlestick makers, not you, and chances are they've sold all their candlesticks and are living in the dark, which accounts for their incredulous suggestion.

These recognized markers fall into that category of analog and digital signals mentioned in *Reading Virtual Minds Volume I: Science and History*. The digital signal, the spoken or written or otherwise communicated word, can be misinterpreted. The markers are the analog signals which tell us which way the ones and zeros of the digital signal portend. Markers in the animal kingdom always tell the truth. With humans, special and extensive training can mask but never completely remove a marker from its place in communication because markers aren't just physical (the nod of the head, the wave of the hand) but also auditory, olfactory, tactile, kinesthetic, ..., and cover all of the sensory modalities.[40,42,72-74,136,144,147,152,180,230,288,382,401,426,482,574] Sociopaths and people with process schizophrenia (such as mentioned in *Reading Virtual Minds Volume I: Science and History*[n]) find it much easier to mask markers because they either were denied social play or experienced repeated trauma in it. This doesn't happen in the animal world where the function of social play is to ensure survival of the group. Cheaters – those who use markers inappropriately – are unlikely to be chosen for play. This becomes a self-fulfilling prophecy on the playground where some children may not be chosen to participate due to awkwardness, speech impediments, lack of "correct" clothing (do they wear

---

[n] – And have I mentioned that great tome is available at Amazon and most discriminating booksellers? http://nlb.pub/RVMV14th

power-ties in schools?) or other oddities. Young canid A who cheats has difficulty getting young canid B to play with it because B can simply refuse to play and choose others in the pack. Young children are not young canids and the pack can ostracize them at will with little regard for its survival in the wild. These children, ostracized, learn to mask their markers in order to survive and become the sociopaths and process schizophrenics of tomorrow.

But when the correct markers are correctly exchanged? The result is trust, and specifically trust that whomever you're exchanging markers with will maintain the rules of the game, that they will play fair.[12,27,29,30,39,46,52,169,224,237,238,263,277,281,304,315,324,348,360,372,399,404,444,514,537,538,585,586,614,618] That game can be softball or tag, international finance or non-nuclear conflict. It is when one party doesn't believe that the other party will play fair, will maintain the rules of the game or changes the rules in mid-game, that all havoc ensues because – you guessed it – a fair-exchange has either failed to take place or was violated while in process. Readers are correct that it is social play and fair-exchange which presage cooperation and reciprocity in society.

A problem currently under investigation by NextStage and others is the increasing lack of fair-exchange between corporations and consumers.[75,83,85,92,112,114,158,519,612] Thus far this longitudinal study has proved the old saying of "Fool me once, shame on you. Fool me twice, shame on me." Consumers are willing to accept that they misunderstood a specific corporation's markers once but not twice, with the mediating factors being quality of service and cost of goods or services to the consumer. Things currently under investigation in this study are whether or not consumers require specialized training in a given industry's markers in order to accept the markers of any individual organization or corporation in that industry. Since the *Reading Virtual Minds* series began, Dell, Comcast and several others have learned the social cost of non-Fair-Exchange behavior.

An example of this is the investment industry. Not everyone should be allowed to invest their own money. For that matter, not everyone should be allowed to drive their own car. An example which comes and goes with the US housing market is the first time home buyer being told a home is "up to code". Buyers from around the country offered that they thought "up to code" meant the construction met some relatively high standard and cite the "up to" part of the phrase as leading them astray. A house being "up to code" merely means it meets the minimum requirements for livability as determined by the local housing authorities. The difference between "up to" indicating a high standard and actually indicating a minimum requirement has lead many first home buyers to rethink whether or not they got a fair-exchange. A response to consumers' concerns is increasing *transparency* in corporations.[7,8,26,68,75,148,158,174,223,227,231,251,327,371,416,422,479,584]

Fair-exchange's great advocate is the return of the sharing economy[28,59,204,207,296,330,376,577] because "this costs that" forms of exchange go out the window. Sharing economies occur when the cost of ownership (along whatever vectors you'd care to consider) is prohibitive but the cost of distributed use is not. Example: I may not need a three-story ladder often enough to purchase one, but you have one and you're not using it this weekend so you'll share it with me. I have two guitars, can only play one at a time and you'd like to play one this weekend and I share it with you. The larger sharing systems involve community ownership, such as shared garden lots and tools in a park. Many times sharing economies evolve around peer-to-peer relationships.°

But peer-to-peer relationships are what anthropologists call class lines, kinship lines, group lines, tribal lines and the like.[177,195-197,199,264,320,332,334,339,342-344,380,383,456,508] Sharing is so completely understood in tribal societies that it is the rule and the modern concept of ownership doesn't exist. Arctic dwellers understand sharing economies and fair-exchange so well that rarely will someone think of an item as lost or stolen, only borrowed and yet to be returned. If I have a better long distance bow than you do, you're going hunting on the barrens and I'm away, you'll take *that* bow (not *my* bow) without thinking or asking.

° – Note that sharing economies are not barter economies. Sharing economies place value on use, not item.

Take-Away #4 – Convince your audience/market/ users that you're just like them and they'll use your product/service/offering no matter how bad it is

Take-Away #5 – Convince your audience/market/ users that you're just like them and they'll help you improve your horrible interface into a high-use one[p]

Anthropology teaches us a great deal about sharing economies. We don't share with people we don't know unless we recognize selfness and sameness. Anything else and the deal won't go through. Con-artists the world over know that to swindle millions from millionaires you have to convince the millionaires that you're a millionaire. You don't have to have millions in reality, all you need do is demonstrate that you're a millionaire and demonstrating that you're a millionaire actually only costs about $20-25k. How come millionaires would never think of giving a million dollar bills to a million poor people but wouldn't hesitate to give a million dollars to another millionaire who has an idea of how to help poor people? And why do con artists con the wealthy and not the poor? Strangely enough, Sutton's Law[q] doesn't apply. Con artists don't con the wealthy because that's where the money is, they con the wealthy because they're easier marks, as in William Parkhurst's "If you know what you're doing, it is far easier to con the rich than the middle class or poor."[r]

Fair-exchange exists in tribal and peer-to-peer societies because entitlement, obligation and their like can't while choice must, and all is based on shared social markers. An obligation to act a certain way destroys fair-exchange and replaces it with

---

[p] – Note in that last Take-Away that the transition is from horrible to high use, not ugly duckling to swan. However, it's also necessary to note that the above take-away demonstrates crowdsourcing in the development community.
[q] – Willie Sutton supposedly said that the reason he robbed banks was because that's where the money was. - https://en.wikipedia.org/wiki/Sutton%27s_law
[r] – http://nlb.pub/Y

resentment in one form or another (everything from jealousy to pride *in* – not *of* – ownership). Entitlement destroys fair-exchange because the give and get are not balanced along mutually accepted axes. But choice? The choice to act or not, to participate or not, to share or not. Mutual choice is fair-exchange's friend and guardian. When we both act and our acts balance, it is because we choose to act in balance. Nobody can feel cheated in a fair-exchange economy, everybody will feel cheated in a market value economy at some point in time. Note this; everybody can feel superior in a fair-exchange, nobody can feel cheated in a fair-exchange. This is one reason fair-exchanges usually exist when the participants share tribal, group, cultural or some other identity while they don't often exist when the participants come from different tribal, group, cultural or other identity cues.

Let me share with you two anecdotes about fair-exchange and social markers missed and excused.

I was in a Tim Horton's™ donut shop on the way to NextStage's Mississauga, Ontario, Canada office. It was morning and there was a good sized line snaking through the tables and chairs. Some people pulled into the parking lot, saw the size of the line and pulled out again. I was three patrons away from the counter when a nice looking fellow in a business suit came in, walked up to me and patted my back in a friendly way. "I'll have a small double-double[s]," he said. I don't know everyone in the Mississauga office so I stared at him, my brow furrowed, attempting to place him.

He laughed and said, "I'm just kidding." I smiled and he took his place at the end of the long line.

I purchased my coffee *and purchased this gentleman a double-double*. I then walked up to him in line and held it out to him with a smile on my face. "Here's your small double-double, friend."

He was shocked. "I was only kidding."

"No problem. My treat. Enjoy."

"Let me pay you, at least."

----

[s] – A coffee with two sugars and two creams.

"Nope. It's a gift. Consider it friendship."

This fellow was so unsettled that he stumbled a bit on his way to sit down. Evidently my generosity had an impact on several people in the store. I didn't recognize his "play" marker. He and others didn't recognize my "play" marker. Fortunately the only thing involved was a cup of coffee.

The second anecdote demonstrates a misunderstood exchange when a great deal more was at stake. I was walking down the halls of a company I once worked for, my boss beside me and the two of us discussing a project we were working on. The CEO of the company was walking down the hall towards us. As he passed we said hello and he did the same.

The difference was that none of the necessary "hello" or "I'm busy and this is a courtesy acknowledgement" markers were present. Many other markers were present – "no one must know", "I'm going to leave here" among others – and I stated them clearly, "You're planning on selling the company, aren't you? In two months, I think."

Needless to say there was no indication that a sale of the company was in the offing. The CEO, however, didn't laugh or simply shake his head, no. He turned on me, red-faced, shouting and eyes bulging. "How did you know that? Who told you?"

How do people of different group/tribes/gender/economic status engage in a fair-exchange when identity cues are not shared? There are two basic ways. The first is easily demonstrated by toddlers when they first meet other, unknown toddlers, is more culturally known from StarTrek™'s "First Contact" scenarios and is based on the First Rule of Semiotics: The first communication must be instructions on how to build a receiver.[t]

The second way is more common and deals with what we do when we want to share but don't have selfness and sameness cues – the shared tribal, group, cultural, et cetera, markers – from the other party, when we want to act but do not understand

---

[t] – Extra points to readers who can solve that without a background in semiotics. The first rule is usually the determinator of how far someone will progress in their studies and the field in general.

or have access to the other party's choice, and want to be sure we're superior or at least equal and not cheated.

We rely on negotiators. Agents. In the mobile world, we rely on apps. Airbnb, Uber, Peerby and Lyft are all examples of negotiators that we've placed our trust in. Note that, not the person we're sharing with, but with the app performing the negotiation.

2 – Negotiating a Fair-Exchange

More often than not our modern forms of ritual tattooing shared identity markers goes beyond clothing and involves speech patterns and language usage[17,18,34,36,90,185,187,194,209,283-286,295,314,331,367,476,489,495,512,518,525,562,565,579,610,616] on down to how we make things discoverable on the 'net.[24,163,208,233,350,391,448,453,546,556,589,592,595,608] In all cases, we're relying on some agent to negotiate a fair-exchange with a partner we have little direct knowledge of.

2.A – Speech and Language

The boon of speech patterns and language usage is that we carry those tribal markers with us even when we don't carry others. You can be naked in a locker room shower surrounded by others equally naked and recognize the different professions by a turn of phrase and the jargon being used.

But what happens when two people meet and they don't use the same speech patterns and language cues, can't see each other to determine if the correct tribal markers are being worn or demonstrated, and can't communicate in the usual ways in order to establish each other's affiliations?

Well, then it's time for a negotiator, an individual adept at communicating to both participants using each's own tribal identifiers with the goal of getting each participant to recognize that the exchange between the two is fair and a "good trade".

Today (and probably moving forward) the negotiator is going to be an electronic interface and the good trade is going to be information-based.[a] We are in a knowledge economy[504] and the currency is information (oh, that it were wisdom!) more than it has ever been before. More accurately,

---

[a] – A characteristic of both Shannonistic and Semiotic information is that it is energy bound, meaning evolution once again rears its head in communication.

- the negotiator can't require more information from either party than they're willing to give to each other and
- *the negotiator must be transparent to the exchange process*.

Take-Away #6 – The minute your interface gets more of the user's attention than what the user wants to get done, your interface has failed

The moment the negotiator's presence is recognized by either party the fair-exchange is no longer between person A and person B; there are now two exchanges being enacted, one between person A and the negotiator and a completely unique and separate exchange is going on between person B and the negotiator. Now-a-days we have special terms for these triangulators: we call them agents and attorneys. They can be real estate agents and attorneys, sports agents and attorneys, book agents, studio agents, record agents, ... An obvious outcome of a "negotiator" in a social setting is to create a network (LinkedIn, Facebook, Twitter, et cetera, are all social negotiators in the guise of social networks). Many people have had the experience of introducing one friend to another friend, having the two friends hit it off well and the "negotiator" – the person who made the introduction – then going unnoticed as the two friends create a bond stronger than the negotiator had with either. This is an example of networking behavior where strong links supersede weak links in interactions. Depending on whose point of view is referenced, this either is or is not a fair-exchange. Sometimes the function of the negotiator is to set the framework in which a strong link can take hold. Many cultures encourage the social networks created by such negotiators at selected points in their children's lives. These negotiators are known as marriage brokers.

The role of the agent is that of a specialized negotiator. "I'll have my agent call your agent." "I'll have my attorney talk to your attorney." "Have your people call my people." We remove ourselves from the fair-exchange and admit our ignorance, admit that our innate sense of what's fair might not be up to the task, and look for a negotiator to take our place.

The problem in sacrificing yourself to a surrogate is that the function of a recognized negotiator is expediency, not equality, and that the expediency might be for later in the exchange, not now.[b] Negotiators may have your best interests at heart but the agent who tells you to settle for less or ask for more than you want in a negotiation is shaking you to your core. Your concept of fair-exchange, your innate sense of what "this" is worth, is in error and because fair-exchange grows from our core concepts of value it is the Core which is in question, nothing less and nothing more.

Have you ever heard two people talking about a purchase and one says to the other something like "You'll have to explain to me why that's worth that much", "What makes it worth that much?" or "What is it made out of, gold?"? What you're hearing is someone's Core being shifted, and only if they accept the new definition of worth and value. They won't accept the new information in an instant. Usually such shifts require hours if not weeks, months or years in order to work their way in. That's why the person needing the explanation often comes back some time later and says, "Okay, I thought it over and you're right. It is a good value at that price."

Take-Away #7 - The easiest way to shift a consumer's core is to give them what they want first, then demonstrate that the added value is both usable and useful without diminishing the ability to do what they wanted in the first place

Give consumers what they want – even if, to paraphrase the late Steve Jobs, "People don't know what they want until we give

---

[b] – An example of this is "I'm officially too unreliable" anecdote on page 36.

it to them"[170,421] – first and they'll willingly take anything else you offer them as part of the package.[c]

> **Take-Away #8 - The easiest way to get consumers to switch brands is to give them what they want**

And this is where we have the Steve Jobs-Henry Ford intersection. Henry Ford's "If I'd asked my customers what they wanted, they'd have said a faster horse" has meaning in many places and especially here.

> **Take-Away #9 – Excellent design occurs when designers know what consumers want, how that varies from what they ask for, and how to guide them to satisfying their needs within the "Want-Asked For" paradigm**

2.B – Discoverability

Discoverability is a bit trickier to deal with when negotiating a fair-exchange and that trickiness has nothing to due with fair-exchange itself. Discoverability deals with privacy, identity, cybersecurity, marketing, you pick it, it's in there somewhere, and that's what makes discoverability tricky. Discoverability is about how and where you place your content (or pointers there to) so that your audience or market and only your audience or market can find it. Where and how you place your content has a lot to do with your audience and very little to do with your content.

---

[c] – This gets into *Educated Palettes*, as in someone being willing to pay a higher price for a rare wine, a painting, a perfume and so on. First, note that all educated palettes are sensory based and that the senses need to be taught or trained to appreciate the higher priced item. Educated palettes are also why it's easier to con the wealthy than the poor – get them to believe something is rare, fine or better and the con is in – and why children can see naked emperors while others can't.

For example, it's common now-a-days for a potential employer to look through someone's social pages before making a hiring decision. The Drunken Pirate[98,99,497] learned this all too well. It's becoming common for employers to request employees make their social handles, et al, known and will take action for anything they discover that they don't like. To hell with Snowden, WikiLeaks and whistleblowing, don't you think?

How about kids who post things they don't want their parents to know about?

Twelve-Step programs are wonderful examples of social discoverability and identity management. Pseudonyms won't work if you reveal something at a meeting and someone at the meeting knows you on the outside and blabs it to their friends.

Think folks who were using AshleyMadison® were concerned about discoverability? If they weren't, what were they doing on AshleyMadison® and doesn't it suck to be them now?

Even a free and democratic society must deal with discoverability issues. If not, why bother with firewalls, network blocks, passwords and all the rest?

Because I'm happy to share with you but not those folks over there. I want to be known by you but not as well known by them. The joke I tell at home may not be as funny to people who know me less well, and am I being socially sensitive if I don't share it with the latter or just protecting myself from future problems? And if those folks find out I tell those kinds of jokes? Will they feel betrayed? And if so, because I did or didn't take them into my confidence? From *Reading Virtual Minds Volume II: Experience and Expectation* we get "Expectation is based more on context than content" and "The tendency to categorize our sensory environment is the rule".

That's discoverability.

Discoverability's demarcation is at the personal-commercial boundary. Companies want people to discover their products, services and offerings, but not their secret sauce. That's corporate espionage! More correctly, that's identity management with the legal concept of a corporation as an entity.

Not only do companies want selected discovery, they recycle email lists, address lists, phone numbers, contacts, canvassings and more to make sure what they want discovered is discovered by the correct people.

On the personal side, it's a little different (see the discussion of jokelists for an example, page 85). That's also discoverability. How about your personal versus your professional contact lists? Discovery at different levels. Do you accept every LinkedIn connection request? What's your criteria? That's a discoverability level. And do you let everybody find you or only people with selected credentials? What about Facebook? Do you let everybody follow you on Twitter and contact you on Skype or FaceTime or Google Hangouts? Your lists may be identical, they may be different, and in either case what you're demonstrating is your personal levels of discoverability.

What is the demarcation between personal and commercial? Most often, personal discoverability occurs in networks where elements of altruism already exists.

Openness and transparency almost always wins in this internet century!
- Todd Rosholt

3 - Fair-Exchange and Altruism

I mentioned previously that corporations are addressing consumer concerns with *transparency*. Unfortunately, what is offered is transparency and what is sought after is one of the curiosities of fair-exchange, altruism.[10,32,39,47,48,50,63,168,172,173,181, 191,205,206,215,235-237,246,247,256,261,262,277,278,292,297,321,323,325,329,345, 360,369,407,412,419,433,434,439,460,467,468,477,488,493,496,502,531,535-537,553,560, 576,581,588,590,604,605,609] Altruism – the quality of unselfish concern for the welfare of others – is a curiosity in a number of disciplines which deal with social interactions. The question of altruism usually comes out as, "Why should A help B when A won't gain anything by helping B?"

That usual question demonstrates the distance between what companies offer and what consumers want. Consumers want corporations that are equals and peers, corporations think of consumers as commodities (hence the market in email lists, social data, the foraging of "big data" and why some people are hired for their "rolodex"). Corporations are willing to be only as transparent as necessary to keep up commodity values (think back to *discoverability*, page 61). Consumers want to trust but trusting the unseen and unknown is usually called faith and consumer faith that corporations are working towards the communal best is long gone[a]. This is increasingly obvious with younger markets where brands are not part of ego identity. Younger markets are losing the concept of *brand* identity in favor of *useful* identity.

Recent studies have shown that, all else being equal, individual B will be very selective when choosing an A to perform an altruistic act. Given enough data about the possible partners, there are four primary criteria person B will use when choosing person A to help them:

---

[a] – As of 2015, anyway. With recent history holding such corporate and governmental blackmarks as The Exxon Valdez, Bhopal, the BP Gulf Oil Spill, Enron, Edward Snowden and William Binney, ..., it's increasingly challenging for consumers to think of corporations and government as anything other than the idiot cousin or bullying big brother.

1) Community - B will chose an A from within their own community (ie, where an existing social network already exists).
2) Identity - B will chose an A who is most like themselves.
3) Belief - B will chose an A who they believe can complete the task.
4) Reputation - B will chose an A who has a reputation of completing similar if not identical tasks.

Graphically, this becomes

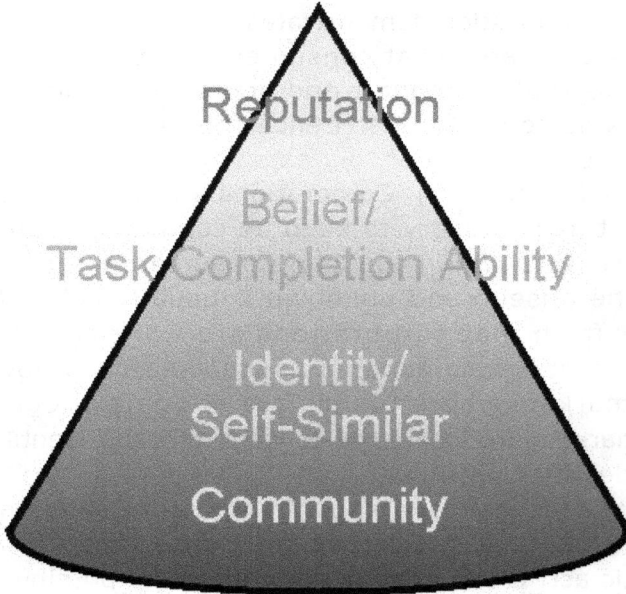

3.1 - Factors are summed from the bottom up. When B seeks an altruistic A, B starts by selecting within their community then proceeds through identity, belief and reputation factors

But what if person B needs some person A to perform an altruistic task and has no immediately available social network?

Then the base of the cone becomes *self-similar* and person B will seek out some person A whom they believe is most like them in some way, shape or form first. That criterion will be followed by *task completion ability* and *reputation*. If there's no available social network and no self-similar individuals? Go to task completion and reputation. No social network, self-similar or task completion candidates? Seek out someone who at least has a reputation for doing such things and ask them. If no elements are available for consideration?

Does this sound like the selection criteria when selecting vendors or what company to partner with? It should.

What's equally interesting is that a selection method exists from A to B, as well. Whenever possible, person A will elect to perform an altruistic act for some person B who

1) Reputation - B already has a reputation for making good of similar if not identical altruistic acts and
2) Belief - A believes B has a better than average chance of successfully completing the overall task that A is helping with and
3) Identity - A believes B shares some aspects, qualities, beliefs, traits, ... (ie, someone whom A perceives as similar to themselves in some way, shape or form) and
4) Community - B is known inside A's social network (ie, from some community individual A is familiar if not comfortable with) and

Graphically, this becomes

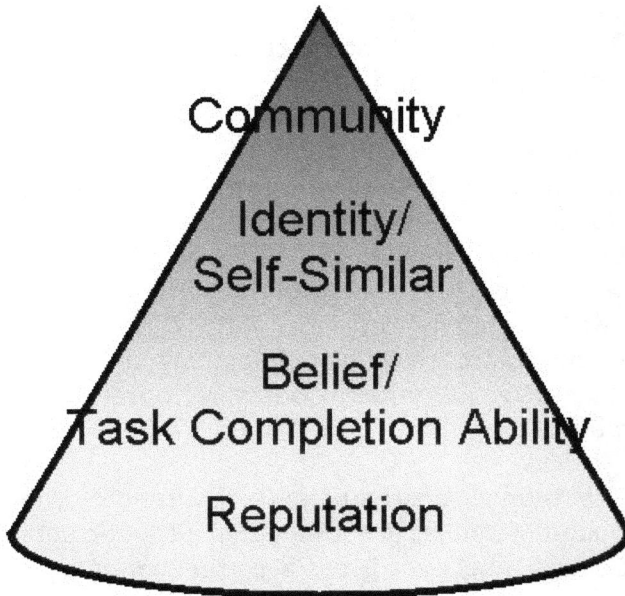

3.2 - Factors are still summed from the bottom up but
they are reversed when A is deciding whether or not to
perform an altruistic act for B

The get method works in reverse order to the give criteria
(yep, fair-exchange again). There is a method (if you will) to this
madness, however; the get method starts with the largest
possible number of participants then works to narrow the number
of participants to those possessing the greatest number of give
criteria. This is where altruism meets social networking. I'll
discuss this meeting of altruism and social networking in more
detail later in *Chapter 5 – Fair-Exchange and Altruism in the
Information Age* (page 84).

There is a curiosity involving the three stages of learn-
ing[16,43,55,64,90,201-203,216,222,251,258,260,269,288,317,319,349,357,393,409, 423-
425,429,452,481,516,521,523,599] as they apply to the social cognition of
altruism. It goes like this:

1 - People will allow their Personality matrix to seek
    altruistic partners based on the four criteria above
    first. No luck? That means the social rules you learned
    growing up no longer apply.
2 - Drop down to the Identity matrix and seek again. Still
    no luck? That means the cultural signs and signals you
    learned aren't working.
3 - Drop down to the Core and try again. At this point,
    however, most people are either displaying fugue or
    hysteria because they can't be themselves in their
    current social setting and that, as they say, can be
    terrifying in the extreme.[61,271,301,522,583] Remember
    that the Core is the last bastion of the self and has no
    defenses of it's own. People who've dropped back to
    their Core are working with only their most primitive,
    emotionally based, what some might call "reptilian"
    brain and mind. We're talking cornered animal here.
    Their basic options are fugue, hysteria or, depending
    on other factors, attack.

Let's provide some examples for this "Search for Altruism"
hierarchy as it applies to grocery shopping and let's start at the
top.

A will chose the individual who has a reputation of
completing similar if not identical tasks.[397,411,483]

You're shopping in your local groceria. You come down one
particular aisle that has some product you need. The product is
on the top shelf and you can't reach it. As you're wheeling your
cart down the aisle, another shopper stops and looks up at the
product you want. This shopper also can't reach the top shelf.
This shopper asks a tall third person to get the product for them,
which this third shopper does.

Whom do you ask to help you get the product, the person
who needed help or the person who gave help? The answer is
obvious, but why so? What if this altruistic third shopper has

retrieved some product from the top shelf for two shoppers prior to your arrival? Do you not ask them? Or do you hurry towards them while calling out "Oh, could you grab one for me, too?" What if you're number five to ask for assistance? What if there's a line and it's obvious the altruistic shopper is growing weary of the game? Do the rules change if the altruistic shopper is a teenager? If you're an adolescent shopper do you defer if the altruist is older, or does digital divisivity[156,312,396,540] (there is evidence that digital devices are making us less interpersonally social or at least differently interpersonally social and is covered in *Chapter 6 – Fair-Exchange, Privacy, Identity and Digital Divisivity*, page 98) kick in, meaning new social mores are forming regarding the giving and getting balance? What if the altruist or shopper come from obviously different socio-economic groups? Can a fair-exchange still take place?

Let's keep the example simple and claim there's only you, shopper 2 and the altruistic shopper 3. Shopper 2 has asked and received and so have you. What has shopper 3 gained from this transaction? There is no reward for shopper 3 from either you nor shopper 2 so this is an altruistic act on shopper 3's part. Or is it? This question is critical in the virtual world because in the real world such situations put our socio-biologic energy in motion.

We are designed to be social creatures and are at our best when we share and no matter what we share – bread, water, air, wine, warmth – we share our emotions with it. From ancient traditions such as Sin Eating to Festivals of the Dead, from birthing and marriage ceremonies to initiation rites ranging from hunts to first menses to first time driving a car or grooming your own horse, we are at our best, our worse and all points in between when our emotions are conveyed with our actions through sharing behaviors which themselves are learned during shared social problem solving. When our marketing ignores emotional intent we are denying our social selves a point of contact between provider and audience, and that marketing will fail. We help the courteous, smiling person before we help the antagonistic, frowning person.

Now descend to the second part of our cone.

A will chose the individual who they believe can complete the task.

More accurately, *A will chose the individual whose skills most closely match the skill set A believes is necessary in order to complete the task.*[405,537,597] This is known as *trait-selection* and can also be seen in any grocery store. Shorter people ask taller people to get things off the higher shelves for them. The selection process for the altruistic act is the belief that the other person has the necessary traits, abilities, skills, et cetera, to complete the task. I've never seen someone under 5'5" ask someone shorter than them to help reach something that's high up. What I have seen is height-challenged people looking up and down the shopping aisle for someone short-challenged.

Even though the above example is well known and understood, what does the tall person gain from this exchange? Have you ever seen a tall person ask a short person to get something from a bottom shelf for them?[b] To do so would be considered rude, possibly disgraceful, but why? If the tall person gives up some of their time, what do they get in return? They have engaged in an altruistic act, albeit a simple one, and by definition there is no reward. Or is there? Remember this question for later.

Let's up the ante on our *task completion ability* shopping game. The short person doesn't see a tall person, but they do see someone the same height as themselves yet with abnormally long arms, perhaps knee or mid-calf length. Arms long enough to draw attention and not just from a tailoring perspective, someone who would be classified as deformed but not non-functional. The short person hesitates to ask. Why? Because the rules of fair-exchange forbid the question to be asked. Again ask, "why?" Perhaps the answer is "because you'd be taking advantage of someone's

---

[b] – See http://nlb.pub/T for a remarkable example of this type of altruistic exchange with children.

deformity", and this brings us to the next tier in our altruism search cone.

The next tier is

A will chose the individual who is most like themselves.

This deals with the concepts of *stranger* vs *self*[c], what behavioral ethologists call *kin selection*.[21,50,57,173,198,221, 225,244,274,277,289,311,325,341,345,368,407,418,432,433,438,440,471,486,514,526,532,535 ,536,538,539,561,581,605] Research indicates that people select partners for altruistic events based on the recognition of self-similar qualities when task-specific qualities aren't required or are unavailable. This is also demonstrated by our shopping game. Let's say that the short person doesn't need something from a top shelf. Instead our 5'5" shopper wants an opinion on a cleaner, a brand of ice cream or a type of orange. Does our shopper seek out someone over six feet tall or with abnormally long arms? No, more often than not and without realizing what they are doing, our 5'5" shopper will stop someone closer to their height, someone they can "see eye to eye with". "Seeing eye to eye" is well known in psychotherapeutic paradigms. Good counselors will instinctively position themselves so that they're on an eye-to-eye level with their clients during a counseling session and thus look more like their client and less an authoritative, possibly threatening figure (if taller) or inexperienced, possibly ineffective figure (if shorter). The science that evolved out of the study of human kin selection behavior is sometimes called *koinophology*, literally the study of beauty (or at least what different groups consider beautiful).[4,6,9,11,20,37,41,54,58,184,190,192,198,212,213,218,229,234, 240,249,267,293,314,338,340,353,358,374,387,392,400,410,437,441,457,462,465,474,485,499 ,501,506,549,550,558,571,573,583,587,600,603,606,607,615,621,622] Kin selection doesn't limit itself to obvious physical characteristics, however, and is the root of branding. People who have a BMW are more likely to talk to other BMW owners than they are likely to talk to Ford owners and vice versa. People who shop at TheGap™ are

---

[c] – ET recognizes five degrees between deciding someone is a stranger versus someone is the same as you.

more likely to talk to other Gap™ shoppers than they are to talk to people who shop at Frenchy's Discount Clothes. How would they know? The logo on the jeans, jackets, shirts and shoes. Kin selection is based on identity and not personality. In both *reputation* and *task completion ability*, A will accept a helper who they can't identify with if required. In *self-similar*, A wants to know B understands what A is about, wants, or is after.

Take-Away #10 - Design hierarchical (vertical) network applications to reward and recognize task completion or accomplishment

Hierarchical networks are pretty well known and recognized. Any military organization is a hierarchical network architecture. An amusing anecdote about the pervasiveness of hierarchical networks involves the Mercury astronauts' wives. They were all gathered for some press event and were told to line up according to rank. The wives rearranged themselves accordingly.

But according to what? The wives were civilians and not in the military. They had no rank hence couldn't line up according to rank. Such was the pervasiveness of their husbands' hierarchical network.

Another well recognized hierarchical network is just about any male social network.[53,56,118,148,217,255,276,333,361,381,422,450,518,593] It can be a club, a team, a bunch of friends going out for drinks, it doesn't really matter. Here I'll share what happens when male social network hierarchy is misunderstood, ignored, et cetera.

Long ago and far away, I had a serious relationship with a particular woman. She took me home to meet her family. At one point and after a wonderful dinner conversation with her, her parents and two older brothers, her father invited me downstairs for a game of pool and cigars.

I don't know much about pool. I know more about mechanics and ballistics, things that pool is based on. At that time I didn't smoke cigars so refused when one was offered.

First social cue missed - acceptance of a token to establish similarity.

I beat one brother in a close game. I was perfecting my calculations and skill during this game.

Her dad handily beat her other brother. It was no where near a close game.

I now played her dad while her brothers watched. All three were puffing on cigars. I made shot after shot after shot, not paying much attention to them, focusing on each shot and making ballistic calculations. I do remember that their puffing became more pronounced as I finished run after run after run.

At the end of the third game, my eyes still on the table, I said, "Rack them up again?"

The coldness of her father's "No" made me look up. The three of them were staring at me from the other side of the table, father in the center, brother on either side, all three with a cue in their hands, white-knuckle grips on the shafts, bumpers on the floor and tips up around face level so they stared at me over the green of the tips.

They could have been wearing six-guns and saying "Get out of town." The message was that clear.

Second social cue missed - recognition and acceptance of social hierarchy.

One brother stayed downstairs to clean up, the other brother and father marched me upstairs where the evening slid into a miasma of innuendo about my ethnicity, heritage, education, language skills, clothing, financial prowess and so on. The woman later told me that her parents didn't like me and wouldn't accept me into their family.

Lucky me, yes?

Rewarding task completion or accomplishment is something that can be seen any time staff meetings are called, formally at the place of work or informally at a local watering hole, and one person is singled out for an outstanding something or other. The reward can be monetary, ornamental, a pat on the back or a drink purchased by the boss. The important aspect is that the reward is for something done; a deal signed, a contract negotiated, a sale made, an acquisition completed, ..., and that the reward be public.

Take-Away #11 - Design horizontal network applications to reward and recognize compatible peerings

Horizontal networks are sometimes called matrix networks, peer-to-peer networks, and are most often seen in female based social systems. A distinction of true horizontal networks is that they included *peerings*, meaning two or more people are equals even though they may not be at the same level. There may be recognized leaders and leadership flows as specific skills are needed by the network. Because leadership flows, two people whom society recognizes as distinctly different – a janitor and a lawyer – may be a compatible peering because their different skills compliment and augment each other for some specific task (i.e., people are recognized for what they can do and what they've done, not for who they are). More often than not horizontal networks have arbiters – people who keep things running smoothly when there's disagreement – rather than specific leaders. Such networks are team oriented. They may have superstar players and those players truly work for the team, not individual achievement or recognition. Horizontal networks will often form internal clusters, small groups that come together to achieve something or function for a specific purpose. Recognizing these clusters privately is reward in horizontal networks.

What does this have to do with enlisting the aide of someone with long arms to reach something you can't? They are the same, but different. They might be kin, but they might not. You should be able to trust them, but maybe you should not. The deciding factor is found in the base of the cone. Kin selection in primitive societies involves the village. An example is from Barry Lopez's *Of Wolves and Men*:

"The social fabric of the Naskapi tribe is the result of an
acknowledgement of dependence on each other for food.
The young, the old, the sick, they cannot hunt. The social
system of the Naskapi bestows prestige on the successful
hunter; that is what is exchanged for meat. Each man hunts
as he chooses, calling on personal skills, but with a single
overriding goal; to secure food. The individual ego is
therefore both nurtured and submerged. A man's skills are
praised, his food is eaten, his pride is reinforced."[385]

Kin selection in modern, especially western, highly mobile
societies, usually involves the neighborhood which is itself
defined by an uncertain boundary. The 2006 Mother's Day Floods
in Nashua, NH, elicited this response once the waters receded "It
was close, and our neighborhood really pulled together to
sandbag each other's property." The statement was more truthful
than the speaker perhaps intended. The speaker's language
indicates they did not think the neighborhood would pull
together. Indeed, the community effort made regional news. Not
terribly long ago a community pulling together during an
emergency would not have been newsworthy, it would have been
expected. It still happens in modern societies but only because
social tools make it easy to do.[108,119,121,529,613]

So why did the neighborhood come together? People could
have seen to their own needs, saved their own homes. Instead
they worked as a unit to assess threats and respond as needed.
This gets us into the area of individuals who choose not to take
part in altruistic behavior when asked.

*The difference between successful
people and very successful people is
that very successful people say no to
almost everything.*
— Warren Buffet

4 - Fair-Exchange and Non-Altruistic Behavior

In the early 1980's I came out of a grocery store and wheeled my cart to my car. Next to my car was another car with a late-middle aged woman putting groceries in her car. A young man (I learned he was twelve years old) quickly came up to her and asked if she needed help putting groceries in her car. She did and so he helped her. He then asked if she'd like him to take her cart back into the store. She said "Sure, go ahead," and quickly turned away, got in her car and drove off. As she drove off the boy pushed the cart to the cart corral and started looking for someone else to help.[a]

During the young man's approach I observed the woman's posture change, her face stiffen and anticipated the drama about to unfold. I waved him over and said I didn't know the store offered that kind of assistance. It didn't, he said. He and a few friends did this to make some money on tips. He smiled at me when he said the word "tips". I then noticed a few other young men performing the same service around the lot. How did it go for them?

It turned out it went pretty well. They made enough each weekend to get them through the week. He described the rules to me – after I gave him a tip – and it was quite a well defined enterprise. All participants pooled their earnings at the end of the day, there was a reward for the fellow who earned the most, they shared strategies and techniques, lunch money was deducted equally from the end of day totals, they pooled resources when someone came out with several shopping carts full of groceries. Were the same boys always involved in the enterprise? Usually the same players were involved, although once in a while someone couldn't make it and they'd get somebody else to take the spot. Did anyone ever cheat (not give over their money at the end of the day)? Yeah, but those kids were never invited back

---

[a] – I invite readers to do a little self-inspection at this point in the book. Did the anecdote recounted thus far cause discomfort? If so, why? What expectation was placed on the outcome which was supplied from somewhere other than in the text?

and if they did, the regular players hustled that much more to make sure the cheater didn't get much work.

These kids – I doubt if any one of them was over 12 years of age – had worked out a gaming strategy that has only recently been documented in anthropology; they had formed themselves into a *sanctioning institution* because they recognized there was a competitive advantage to punishing non-altruistic behavior.[32, 35,47,179,191,205,236,243,266,277,278,292,297,304-306,308-310,315,324,345, 472,473,533,536,588,602,605] They had learned to create kin based on altruistic principles, then to punish kin who failed in the fair-exchange by ostracizing them from the community. This was self vs stranger ethology in action!

What about when they got stiffed, I asked, such as the scene I'd just witnessed?

It turned out they kept track of the free riders and small tippers. It was a big shopping community and the parking lot was usually three-quarters full. Did they go by license plates? Did they know these people outside the confines of this game?

His answer amazed me and it must have showed because he smiled at my response. His teammates used trait-selection determined over time to isolate and punish free riders and small tippers. It wasn't license plates so much as it was make of car. It wasn't amount of groceries so much as what the groceries were. It wasn't what kinds of clothing they were wearing so much as whether or not the clothing had a designer label and if yes, what the designer label was.

Was this method infallible? Not always. Sometimes they would help someone who fit the deselection criteria and get a big tip. What was the deciding factor to offer help? None of them knew (I offered to pay them to take an afternoon break and buy them milkshakes by this time). There was just something about some people that let you know they were good for the money and others weren't. How come none offered to help me? Did I somehow signal I wasn't good for the money? My original informant said he was watching me. It was a toss up between me and the woman next to me. I popped my trunk and picked up four grocery bags, two in each hand, so I didn't need help.

Another fellow nodded. "And you were walking too fast." Semiotics in action. My signals were not those they associated with a silent and non-conscious request for help. Sometimes one of these players would see an inexperienced teammate moving towards a target whom the more experienced teammate had deselected and signal the novitiate off.

Both the grocery store parking lot anecdote and the Mother's Day Flood anecdote deal with a social network's ability to recognize and punish free riders and minimal contributors.[32, 38,47,63,166,206,236,253,257,278,280,323,324,326,345,359,360,394,397,419,433,477,488, 494,496,502,557,560] In both cases a community is established with the goal of the community being that the community as a whole should prosper. Inclusion in the community is done via kin selection. What is the determining factor in selecting kin? The novitiate's ability to engage in a fair-exchange with others in the community.

Another example of fair-exchange and non-altruistic behavior can be pulled from our pyramid diagrams, figures 3.1 and 3.2 on pages 66 and 68; What happens when someone with a recognizable "prize/gift/bounty/boon" refuses to cooperate? This happens at the apex of the altruism selection pyramid. Someone who has a reputation of completing similar if not identical tasks refuses to complete the requested task. Is this where the Warren Buffet quote that opens this chapter makes itself known?

Remember what is involved in deciding to ask such an individual in the first place; they are not refusing to complete the task, they are refusing to help you. An individual with strong core, identity and personality matrices shrugs, walks away and goes to the next altruistic candidate on the list. The individual lacking strong core, identity and personality matrices?

This individual must again seek self-definition and the best way to seek it is within the individual's community (remember that the individual with the reputation of being able to help exists outside the community by definition). The individual refused help returns to his or her source – both sociologically and psychologically – without the prize and having failed in their quest. They seek solace with others who either also failed or never ventured on the quest at all. Why seek solace there? Why go to others who also failed when it might be wiser to go to others who were successful to learn where one might do better the next time?

Because others who were successful are, by definition, also outside of the refused individual's community and seekers with a strong core, identity and personality will have defined themselves not as "refused" but as "unaccepted as of yet". These latter individuals have also already decided that their original community is not where they belong.

Always, always, always, the goal of the Core, Identity and Personality is to establish itself in some kind of community. If an individual recognizes his or herself as refused then they must willingly sacrifice their quest in order to maintain their social standing/hierarchy and use their failure to sustain/build their community (if you know any business consultants who failed in business and now lecture on business failure, you know such individuals).

The individual who is either successful or not yet accepted has removed him or herself from their original community and moved up the altruism selection pyramid. Also appreciate that they had no choice. Group dynamics kicks in in the original group and, as is recognized in group and family therapy and dynamics, nobody can be healthier than the group is healthy. The pressure to conform to the role the group defines for you is tremendous and is often why individuals have to leave their source communities when they go through a life change (a recovering alcoholic, a religious conversion, et cetera). When the dwarves are for the dwarves[b], it doesn't bode well to be a human.

> **Take-Away #12 – The strongest and best influencers will be those who've already travelled the neophyte to boon cycle and preferably more than once**

---

[b] – from C.S. Lewis' *The Last Battle*, the final *Chronicles of Narnia* book.

Take-Away #13 – A community will self-elect and self-correct influencers based on kin and trait selection

Take-Away #14 – Paid and company selected influencers will be given obligatory attention at first then ignored by the community once their selection status is recognized

I appreciate your opinion that the digital realm is not intended to replicate offline experiences, since such a thing isn't really possible (though much of the world seems to think it is not only possible, but essential). I've always found it funny that the marketing world collectively believes something impossible to be a requirement.
— Susan LeBlanc

5 - Fair-Exchange and Altruism in the Mobile Era

We now come to online altruism, an area where the Core is active because we create and destroy identities and personalities online, in the virtual world, all the time. The person who has one email account for personal emails, another as gatekeeper for unknown business, yet another for known business (reminiscent of asking someone's phone number and they scribble something down, saying "This is my direct line. Please don't give it out."[109] You know you've entered the *sanctum sanctorum*, been given the keys to the kingdom and so on. Give out the keys of entry and you've violated a sacred trust, demonstrated you are not kin and will not act altruistically in the community. You are, in short, a *cheater*[32,63,236,345,360,419,488,496]), and still one more for receiving list-server emails is creating personalities to suit virtual realities they hope to inhabit. The move from the desktop to the mobile signals the move from multiple email accounts to multiple mobiles. Brings a whole new meaning to "I told you not to call me at this number," doesn't it?

Most of us still recognize a difference between the real and the imaginary (virtual) worlds we live in. How do the pyramids in figures 3.1 and 3.2 on pages 66 and 68 apply? Is there overlap from one virtual reality to the next?

One thing that is well known about altruism is that it most often occurs when communities – social networks – have already been established. The concept of kin selection and selfness extends itself to people who are alike in some way, shape or form. The fact that I, for example, am part of some social network predicates that my first choice for enlisting someone else in altruistic behavior will be someone from that social network. That social network can be my next door neighbor, someone I see daily while walking my dog, someone I see often at the gym, someone I know is from New Hampshire, someone I know is from the USA[a], someone I know is from planet Earth. In today's virtual world, that someone else I enlist in some altruistic behavior might well be someone I've only met in cyberspace.

But if my community is comprised of those whom I only know online, what form does altruism and fair-exchange take?

I posed some questions along these lines in earlier chapters. In all cases, the questions took the form of "What does the altruistic individual gain from their altruistic behavior?" Here we have some answers and the answers have to do with social networking. For our example we're going to use a social networking stalwart of the information age, the joke list.

Most people with email accounts have a least one which they use to send and receive jokes. If you regularly get jokes from people in your email then congratulations, you're on a joke list and joke lists come under the heading of social networks. They also have a lot to do with fair-exchange and altruism, as we're about to see.

I get jokes from people in all walks of life, some I've never met yet have excellent online relationships with and some I've known in person for years. That latter distinction is important. The only way information – jokes – can spread through a social network is if fair-exchange takes place. For fair-exchange to take place there must be trust between the participants and trust comes from the giving and receiving of social value. When all these things are in play it is known as *viral marketing*[b].

Jim Meskauskas[c] wrote on that viral marketing campaigns are really online versions of word-of-mouth (WOM) advertising.[406] If you remember the *Jesus Christ SuperStar* lyric "What's the buzz, Tell me what's a' happening", you know what WOM and viral campaigns are all about.[91,93,94,113,167,214,259,268,379,395,404,406]

---

[a] – People in the USA accepted the surge in fuel costs which were recognizably due to the devastation of New Orleans' and the Gulf's infrastructure, and that acceptance can be thought of as altruistic behavior. Essentially, A was willing to suffer (pay higher fuel costs) because B was already suffering (the devastation). Flash forward to the record oil company profits of 1Q06 and the people are nearer revolt. How come? Because the first was a fair-exchange, "They're suffering so I can suffer." The second doesn't involve a recognizable fair-exchange so people feel violated, their trust betrayed, and are more demonstrably upset.
[b] – http://en.wikipedia.org/wiki/Viral_marketing
[c] – https://www.linkedin.com/in/jim-meskauskas-1b988

Meskauskas offered four items that good viral marketing campaigns share:

- Entertainment - the marketing is entertaining
- Utility - what is being marketed is something the reader can use
- Palpable reward - the marketing provides instant gratification
- Uniqueness - the marketing is like nothing the reader has ever seen

He also describes the difference between frictionless and active viral marketing. Frictionless occurs when the audience spreads the good word via usage (you see me doing something, I'm enjoying myself, you give it a try), active viral marketing occurs when the audience spreads the word via actively recruiting non-audience members into the audience ("I'll put you on my jokelist").

Joke lists, spam and viral marketing rely on social networks in order to function.[76,78] Let's consider Jim Meskauskas' four bullets as they apply to something nobody wants – spam – something people willingly accept and often look forward to – jokes from known associates – and how the rules of viral marketing make each one what it is.

Joke lists address all four of Meskauskas' bullets. They provide entertainment, there is instant gratification hence a palpable reward and they offer the individual something they've never seen before. I'll hold off on their utilitarian aspect for now.

Joke lists are also examples of active viral campaigns and the social networks which empower them. Someone read the joke or followed the link because it was sent to them, they laughed, they then sent it onto me, I laughed, now I'm now sending it onto you in the hopes that you'll laugh.

Spam doesn't hit any of Jim Meskauskas' four bullets...or does it? James McKim, longtime Chairman of SwANH/NHHTC, said that "...spam is in the eye of the beholder. It all depends upon timing and circumstances of the recipient." His example is looking for airline tickets to take his family to visit his parents. "Most of the year I would consider emails from Orbitz, Travelocity, Priceline, et cetera spam. However, the time of the year when I'm planning my trip, I would not consider them spam." Here is Meskauskas' Utility bullet writ whole and large, but not the other three. Spam often attempts to mimic social networking with subject lines like "You're going to love this" or "Fwd: Funny" or "Fred Derf said to send you this" and so on.

Why do jokes pass the social network filter but spam does not?

Trust, pure and simple.

I trust the people who send me jokes to send me stuff that I'll enjoy. Senders of spam want to fool me into thinking the email is being sent by someone I know and trust (this is also why email accounts are hacked and used to send spam. The spammer/hacker's hope is that you'll click on the enclosed link or open the attached file because you trust the sender). Trust,[176] especially internet trust as it applies to a social network, is a critical element in all marketing and viral marketing in particular because we haven't always met the person suggesting we click on the link embedded in the file. Here's where the distinction between met and unmet correspondents comes in. We trust the person we've never met and have only interacted with electronically to recognize and practice a fair-exchange with us. Fair-exchanges are increasingly recognized as market drivers in neuroeconomics[30,235,430,520] and are why some campaigns work and others fail miserably, why some social networks thrive and others die horrible deaths and why some jokes go round and round and others are seen once and never again.

> **Take-Away #15 – You must give higher quality information to consumers in order to get higher quality information from consumers (want their direct line? give them something that demonstrates you value their time and are worthy)**

How can we develop trust when, historically, trust has been based on a series of face-to-face fair-exchanges?

We develop trust in non face-to-face exchanges by demonstrating Meskauskas' fourth quality, Utility. Utility is the grease on the wheel of non face-to-face social exchanges because *if* you give me something I can use I'll return the favor in two ways:

1) I'll give you something you can use and
2) *I'll trust you to give me something I can use again.*

Note that both of these are the bases for functional behavioral and routing networks (why your friends are your friends rather than simple acquaintances). Using our previous examples, you'll go from the gatekeeper email to the higher access email account, you'll go from "have your people call my people" to "Here's my direct line, please don't give it out." Utility is where the giving and receiving of value occurs, social and otherwise.

I know many of the people on my joke lists pass the jokes on to someone else. This is "Gifting" to cultural anthropologists.[183, 304,567,596] Gifting has different aspects in different cultures. In western culture Gifting's meaning is highly utilitarian, extremely simple and functions to create *social collateral* – my value to you increases because I gave you something you can use and/or will value and don't require its return. Keep me around because I may do this again.

Ah, the social network is formed, a viral campaign succeeds, and the reason for an individual's altruistic act – especially in the virtual world – is revealed; greater access, quicker access, and more importantly a satisfactory glow to and reinforcement of the Core, Identity and Personality matrices. By establishing utility, we establish trust and by establishing trust – the recognition and reinforcement of who we think we are – we open the doors for fair-exchange.

Take-Away #16 – Gifting in app culture takes the form of providing non-interface changing upgrades automatically (make sure they're completely debugged!) then sending a personalized email notifying the user such has occurred

So how do online businesses make use of social networks and fair-exchange? Let's start with Jim Meskauskas' four points; Entertainment, Utility, Palpable Reward, Uniqueness. These are critical and must occur in psychological equal measure. "Psychological equal measure"? Yes, something in the virtual world must have utilitarian value in order for me to propagate it via my social network because my social value (trust, fair-exchange) within that network increases when I pass it on.

The Viral Marketing Pyramid

5.1 - The Viral Marketing Pyramid

Viral marketing and the online social networks which drive them aren't about products or value in the traditional sense, it's about trust and fair-exchange and is pyramidal in structure (as shown in figure 5.1 on page 89). The base is Jim Meskauskas' four elements of Entertainment, Utility, Palpable Reward and Uniqueness. The top of the pyramid is Success (the prize, the boon, the gift, the reward, ..., the crown of the altruistic act). The more you fill that pyramid with Trust and Fair-Exchange the greater your chances are for achieving success. The message to companies going down this road is a simple one.

Take-Away #17 - Make the social value of the exchange more important than what's being exchanged and your campaign will take off every time

Having stated the above, why do so many online businesses fail to create branded social networks or only succeed in creating non-optimal social networks? Because the online world doesn't exist in the same time frame as do face-to-face social networks. Trust and fair-exchange allow social networks to grow. Reputation – the first criteria for selecting an individual for an altruistic act and the last selection method for the same – is built on trust, but trust isn't a spectrum which is distrust to trust (-100 to 100, for example) it is a spectrum from 100% pain to 100% pleasure and the slider is trust itself, as in you trust an individual to cause you pain (what is usually termed as *distrusting* someone) or cause you pleasure (you *trust* someone). This is shown in figure 5.2 on page 90.

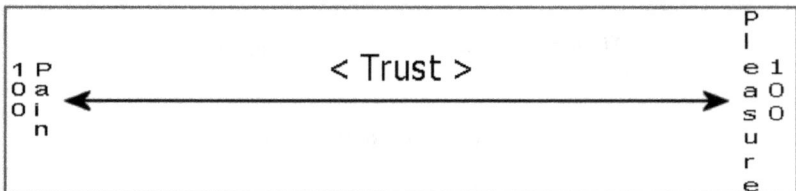

5.2 - "Distrust" occurs in language, not in the mind, because the mind isn't naturally wired to form a negative. You can trust someone to cause you pain, however, and that is what most people define as "distrust".

Trust is closely aligned to *Affinity*, as in you feel an affinity (a social closeness and more correctly *social distance* and *social proximity*) to those you trust. Combine Trust and Affinity and you have the basis of *Reputation*. Trust and Affinity closely aligned and you have the basis of a good, strong social relationship, one which will be proactive to your needs (figure 5.3, page 91), Trust and Affinity misaligned and you have someone you can trust but don't get along with and poor, weak social relationships result, one which will be inactive at best or reactive at worst to your needs (figure 5.4 on page 91).

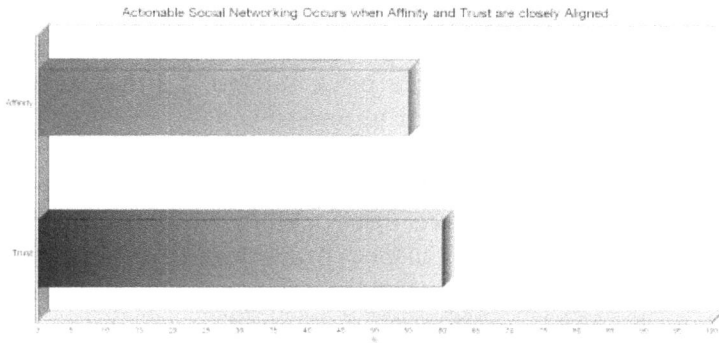

5.3 - Reputation is based on trust (top) and affinity (bottom).
Strong social ties come from trust and affinity being closely aligned

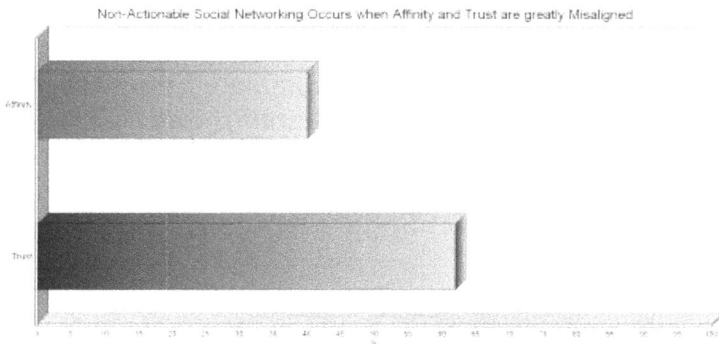

5.4 - Weak social ties and ineffective social networks occur when affinity (bottom) and trust (top) are misaligned. You may trust the person to do good things but have nothing in common with them, hence social ties are weak or non-existent

Reputation is a measure of where someone exists in your psyche on the multi-dimensional pain-pleasure, social distance scale. Someone can have a reputation for causing trouble, therefore you trust them to cause you pain, or someone can have a reputation for beneficence and you'll seek them out to perform altruistic acts. But look further. Someone can have a reputation for beneficence but also being intolerant of bullcrap. You are full of bullcrap and the person knows this. Your affinity to them is quite low even though your trust in them is quite high, and because they have the reputation they have you know the psycho-social price of asking them to help you will be quite high, probably beyond what you're willing to pay, so you seek help from someone more tolerant and less qualified. It all comes down to (again) everything having a price tag on it and you having to decide if you're willing to pay the price.[157]

Strangely enough, these concepts of altruism, fair-exchange, trust, et cetera, are quite active in the online world via behavioral and ad networks. These are networks in which some company monitors the activities of visitors to all sites in their system and shares the so-called behavioral data with everyone.[d] The general consensus, however, is that it's a one-sided game and again, it comes down to the reputation online businesses have garnered in the digital age.

Several online businesses – and especially these behavioral networking businesses – make their living via placing cookies on visitors' computers during browsing sessions. The goal of so doing is to gather enough information so that the business has a better chance of engaging the visitor in a completed transaction. This is a reasonable pursuit in itself and research shows that, given time, fair-exchanges will take place if the business can learn enough about the visitor to offer transactions the visitor has completed in the past.[430] The fair-exchange evolves from a cooperation

---

[d] – NextStage pioneered this concept in 1999-2001, pooling the decision, learning and cognitive styles of visitors across all sites in order to learn what decision strategies were common to all sites. This information was then used to help all client sites improve profitability.

between the business and the visitor in which the first fair-exchange is information.

But this fair-exchange of information is unlikely to occur when the business has a reputation that instills negative trust.[158] What can businesses do to generate positive trust and still gather the information they desire? The solution, originally suggested by NextStage in 2006, is now becoming more and more in vogue; inform the visitor that such cookies are being used and to use them to directly and immediately benefit the visitor. IngentaConnect (figure 5.5, page 93) informs the visitor that cookies are used[e] to help the visitor achieve their goal and how.

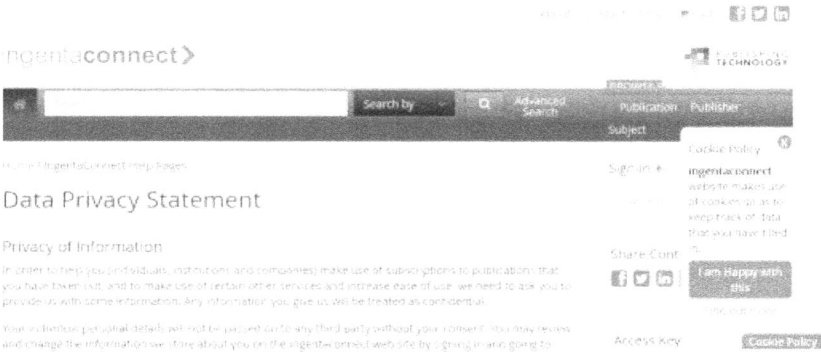

5.3 Ingenta's users' acceptance of cookies has more to do with popup than the policy

This would make cookies fall under the heading of useful viral tools and, if the online business was willing to use these cookies to create social networks which directly benefited the visitor, businesses wouldn't have to worry about people deleting cookies from their computers, a common "viral" plague of the early to mid 2000s. Instead, you'd lose business if you took the cookies away. Consider the following from *A Little About Cookies*:[86]

> An example of cookies being useful to the consumer can be found in my IMediaConnection *Usability Studies 101* columns, *Making Cookies from Breadcrumbs*.[77] Here

---

[e] – This is now law in some countries.

cookies are placed on a visitor's computer to aide them in navigation when they return to the site. For example, someone navigates through a complex and content-rich site, bookmarking a page or two along the way when something triggers an *aHa!* for them. The problem is the page they bookmarked is where they had the *aHa!*, not the page that gave them the *aHa!* and now they're getting frustrated because they can't find the *aHa!* page. Cookies made from breadcrumbs is a useful tool for keeping prospects and clients engaged with and on a site when frustration might drive them away.

Another example of cookies benefiting consumers has nothing to do with cookies per se, but a great deal to do with the explanation of cookies. The challenge to the industry is to make cookies acceptable to consumers. Here I'll paraphrase quantum physicist Fritz London; The real problem of using cookies is not in the public understanding what they are and how they're used, but in the public's not understanding the large and complicated apparatus used to measure them.

First the industry needs to help the public understand that large and complicated apparatus, not the cookies used therein. On homepages and where it can be clearly seen, offer a single paragraph that does three things:

And we'll list them as Take-Aways because they've caused minimum double-digit increases on a number of properties

Take-Away #18 – State that you use cookies, what is captured, how long it is maintained and where it is stored both locally and remotely

Take-Away #19 – State honestly and without marketing jargon the economic and social benefit to the consumer by allowing the use of cookies on your site

Take-Away #20 – State honestly and in neither marketing jargon nor alarmist language the

economic and social detriment to the consumer by not allowing the use of cookies on your site

Two key items to getting the widespread acceptance of cookies, GPS tracking, identity matching and whatever technology comes after them are going to be trust and affinity. The industry wants to build relationships, loyalties and reputations. The keys to all three are trust and affinity. I'm not stating anything new here and I am offering some solutions. Getting consumers to do something the industry wants is much easier when the consumer has a stake in the same goal. Once consumers are comfortable and recognize a given identification technology brings them *direct and obvious value* all such discussions will be moot. You won't be able to get consumers to delete *their* cookies from *their* computers or shut off tracking apps at all because a fair-exchange will be established.

I think moving forward the question becomes "Will businesses be good fair-exchange partners?"

That is a complex question. "Fair-exchange for whom? For what? With what?" A fair-exchange with their shareholders? Then the monies invested are exchanged with the hope of a large reward. Is that a reasonable fair-exchange?

With their customers? Then the monies are exchanged with the hope of reliable goods and services.[158]

With their partners? Probably same as above but with a slightly different fit.

Can any one entity engage in so many fair-exchanges and satisfy all parties on all sides? This is the Core (and I use that term intentionally) question. To survive at all, any organism must make compromises – with its environment, with itself, with others of its kind – but the concept of fair-exchange involves a steadfastness of character for the duration of the exchange that usually doesn't allow much wiggle room. Most people and definitely most businesses don't recognize that "the duration of the exchange" continues until both parties publicly declare the exchange is finished. It's rare that a business will offer a life-time guarantee anymore because they want the exchange to end predictably, not accidentally. Couples may break up and often it's because one partner's character has changed too much and the exchange is no longer fair.

My hope is that compromise and fair-exchange will graph as Minkowski's cones[f] the past as an ever narrowing path, the future an increasing probability and both meet at an irreducible now at which all parties, by now's very irreducibility, will emerge satisfied if not happy.

---

[f] – from *Reading Virtual Minds Volume II: Experience and Expectation* (http://nlb.pub/RVMV21st):
There's a difference between how people think of something and how people demonstrate their experience of that thing. The latter, the demonstration of an experience, is much closer to their Core because it's (often) non-conscious.273 The former, how someone thinks, requires two important factors: education and self-awareness. Without the education and self-awareness, thinking will never influence the Core. However, the Core will always influence how we think.

Whatever I write about the Internet will be outdated in 6 months!
– Melinda Blau, 30 Jul 2009

6 - Fair-Exchange, Privacy, Identity and Digital Divisivity

Starting in early 2010, NextStage began documenting a shift in people's concept of fair-exchange. This shift arrived when the first fully digital generation[12,36,56,62,65,160,186,279,316,336, 381,464,465,487,551,564] was entering the work force, the first generation that didn't know a world without the internet and who had come into maturity with the internet. Some researchers declared that the internet had changed how the brain processes information.[66,547] Several people asked me about this. Did the internet invalidate what I'd been doing for so much of my life?

If it had. I could rest.

The truth is that how the brain processes information is fixed by evolution, anatomy, biology, chemistry, physics and so on. Our auditory centers will still process auditory information. The brain doesn't grow new structures and discard old ones because music has changed from tribal drumming and ritual singing to Georgian chants to Baroque ensembles to modern jazz to *The Voice*. What we appreciate may change and that has more to do with education than changes in neurophysiology. People may think Pollack's a hack and a flea market velvet Elvis the epitome of good art. Both are correct and it's the same parts of the brain making the decision for each of them. *Rex Goliath Free Range Red* is as good as *Armand De Brignac Brut* if you've never been educated in what's what in wines, but the same gustatory, olfactory, tactile and visual sensory systems send the same signals to the same parts of the brain no matter who you are. The only real difference is how you've been taught to interpret those signals (a reference to *Educated Palettes*, page 61).

What is also true is that the brain is incredibly elastic, meaning it can shift and change what it does, reroute neural pathways due to illness or trauma, even restructure itself. The technical term for this is *neuroplasticity*.[186,216,220,475,543,555] People who've lost or damaged their vestibulary sensory system, for example, can learn to balance themselves by training their gustatory and auditory sensory systems to take up the task. It's work and it's doable.

One thing the brain does too rapidly for us to recognize is decide how to handle information. Is this information primarily visual? Send it to the occipitals. Is it primarily auditory? Send it to the auditories. The brain determines if information is future oriented, taste oriented, emotionally oriented, et cetera, and routes it accordingly.[a] What the internet, mobile technologies and the ever popular "internet of things" is doing is inundating us with information, not changing what parts of the brain processed that information.[2,13,14,45,79,82,84,97,101,103-107,110-112,117,129,155,182,200, 239,241,254,299,322,337,352,355,370,377,384,388,390,401,413,415,451,455,484,498,500, 503,505,511,527,548,558,566,617]

Here's what's amusing about the concept of "...inundating us with information". Barry Lopez wrote "No one is quite as alert as an indigenous hunter who is hungry."[386] Anthropologists are overwhelmed when they discover how much information the average indogene is processing at any given moment. But the average indogene is processing information because if they stop they die; a predator will take them, the environment will take them, an enemy will take them and the cues and clues they recognize and respond to is truly inundating to the "modern, educated" mind, and it should be; modern people have delegated much of their survival requirements to city, state and national authorities. We accept that our neighbors will not go ballistic and run us over or shoot us. Modern society relies on these concepts being accepted and that we act as if they're true.

Imagine having to hide from predators and enemies while analyzing the topography, geography and horizon for environmental cues *and then* your mobile pings you with a TXT. Now that's overwhelming information.

---

[a] – From *Reading Virtual Minds Volume II: Experience and Expectation* (http://nlb.pub/RVMV21st): Basically, once people get used to doing something a certain way they become less vigorous with each repetition. The first time somebody does something, the action is "new". The second time, "less new" and eventually the action becomes known and requires less neural effort and energy to perform the action. Have you ever looked at a picture and couldn't figure out what it was, then once told, couldn't stop seeing what you were told it was? That's adaptation method working.

So the brain doesn't do things differently, it simply uses what it has for different things. Again, neuroplasticity at work.

And this brings us to fair-exchange in the age of *digital divisivity*.[12,15,25,36,44,56,153,154,160,248,258,265,275,279,315,347,356,362,364,373, 387,402,416,428,464,465,509,564,568,594,611,618] NextStage first noticed digital divisivity while conducting some research about privacy and identity[b]. It showed up in unrelated conversations regarding identity theft and insurance. Research participants who were thirty-five and older purchased insurance *in case* they have an accident. Participants under thirty-five (and this research was a while ago. The breakpoint is probably 37.5 or even 40 now) purchased insurance *for when* and often *because* they'll have an accident. The slight shift in language is significant and reveals incredible amounts about participants' psyches. The *possible* has become *probable*. In fact, it has become almost definite.

But if I start with the assumption that accidents are going to happen, that they're simply parts of life, my responsibility for avoiding them is minimized. The most horrifying events are no longer improbable, now they're inevitable and there's nothing I can do about them except be along for the ride.

But if I'm no longer responsible, who is? In America and increasingly other locales, two factors rise; whomever has the deepest pockets and has some socially recognized connection regardless of their actual involvement in the event.

Talk about a reason to stay away from social networks! Forget privacy, people are willing to give that up in a heartbeat these days. People will have the most intimate conversations on a mobile phone while standing in supermarket checkout lines. But cut in front of them and they go ballistic because you've cost them *time*. Everybody's fighting for time; their own, somebody else's. That's what marketing and attention are all about.

The age breakpoint also appeared when discussing identity theft and it didn't matter if the theft was of your purse, wallet, mobile, your email or bank getting hacked or your favorite store's accounting system. Above the age break and identity theft was

---

[b] – You can see an interview about internet privacy at http://nlb.pub/S

horrible, below the age break and again, it is simply something that happens. Above the break, the expectation was to be an identity theft victim once every eight or nine years. Below the break, every two to three months.

One meaning of this is obvious; privacy and identity are much more fluid than they've ever been before. Fair-exchange, based on privacy and identity concepts, differs above and below the age breakpoint. Exchanges must still be fair and balanced as described earlier in this book.

However, if I know my privacy and identity are forfeit, if part of my *raison d'etre* is that accidents will happen and I'm not responsible, my sense of what is fair and balanced shifts.

Let's go back to our Amerinds and Colonists example. Identity and privacy are loose, nobody's responsible for whatever occurs.

Caveat Emptor is the new balance point. The Amerinds must be responsible for what they got, the Colonists must be responsible for what they got. The giver has no responsibility to the getter, giver and getter interact virtually and may never meet face-to-face at all.

The price of goods starts a steep climb because the reason for returning goods is never questioned. Automobile dealerships botch up repairs and, if the customer complains, bills don't have to be paid because the social backlash would be too great to bear. Customer service takes a nosedive because it's easier to return payment to difficult customers than make them happy. Only the most severe cases go to court because public opinion, which is fleeting at best, is the court of lost revenue and no business can win that case.

And all because we're ruled by the clock.[60,138,157,232,270,287, 435,459,466,491,513,515,572,582] Cost is more a function of time than materials and labor. Consider the shopper standing at the clothing rack in a downtown store. They see something they like and use a mobile app to read the barcode. The mobile app informs them that the same item is available for $10 less one block away and the shopper asks that you match the price. What do you, as retailer, do? What is the fair-exchange.

There is an apocryphal urban legend about just this thing. A woman was shopping somewhere in Manhattan, saw a dress she liked, used an app and learned the same dress was available for a few dollars less a few blocks away. She showed the app's report to a saleswoman and demanded a price match.

The saleswoman took out her own phone, took a picture of the app's result, told the shopper, "Thanks, I've been looking at that dress myself" and then told her manager that she was going out for a few minutes and went off to purchase the dress for herself.

No offer of help, no offer of adjustment, no attempt to match. Digital divisivity and what's mine is yours and what's yours is mine. The sharing economy comes alive because where we spend our lives, increasingly online, requires our offline lives keep up. Tick tick tick.

Let me give you a real-world example of how fair-exchange is shifting (and a true example of Susan's Big Hammer at work). A 2015 PwC study[c] indicated that people weren't going to movie theaters because prices were too high. But over 80% were willing to spend up to twenty dollars more to watch the same movie at home, 41% claimed that movies weren't as interesting as they use to be and almost a quarter of the people studied wanted better movies, period.

What are they doing instead? Going out to dinner, spending time at home, basically doing other stuff *that interests them*, or in the fair-exchange concept, things they believe provide them entertainment value equal to their effort value. Going out to a movie doesn't provide a fair-exchange to an increasingly older population. PwC's own subtitle for the paper is "Movie goers say, 'Give us great content and rethink our experience.'" Study the language used by respondents and you discover experiential time concepts used by older participants. Their time has a value and the sum of the movie going experience (seating, other theater goers, food and beverage prices, plot, acting, storytelling, et cetera) doesn't equal that value. The same holds true for books,

---

[c] – http://nlb.pub/Z

tv shows, relationships, meals out, anything where you give of yourself and expect an equal get in return. Whenever you give of yourself you're giving some form of energy; physical, emotional, spiritual, psychical. Problems arise when whenever what you get doesn't balance with the same forms of energy. The modern world allows for abstractions along these energy axes (and that's why there's such intense debate of "minimum" wage) but our psyches do not unless we're sufficiently primed and that priming comes from culture, history, ethnicity, ... Talk about chasing one's tail!

So who does like the movie going experience? The young, those in the digital divisivity group.

Surprise!

Fair-exchange is increasingly between retailer and retailer, not shopper and retailer. Costs must be competitive because the price of returns is no longer questioned and shoppers are digitally divisive. They're not responsible (in their own mind) for products and services they no longer want or need, even if it's only moments after purchase.

Buyer regret and remorse? Pah. Stop worrying about them. Invest your time and money in return-exchange storefronts. Have you noticed the increasing division between a retail store and an outlet store? First purchase versus repurchase. Vendors won't argue with consumers over a return, they'll simply resell it at a discount, making it available for repurchase.

The increased handling? No problem. It's handled by the increasing price spiral. Tick tick tick.

What else falls out from these concepts? What else changes in someone's psychology if identity is not only fluid but dynamic and one of the basic working principles is that *merde* occurs with regularity?

In a world where mistakes are part of existence and the effort of avoidance is greater than that act of contrition, precision is no longer required. A "1pm" meeting occurs when the necessary players arrive regardless of the time.

But wait, there's more!

Possibly the individual begins insulating themselves against these merdic shocks. Instead of suffering *petite mals* their brain goes to a state of *petite terror*. The only certainty is that things will change. Relationships are no longer stable. Have you ever heard someone say "I stopped seeing him/her because they were too much work"? That's a fair-exchange statement. The person making the statement was not receiving a fair-exchange for their effort to make the relationship work, so quit the relationship.

But that statement can only be made by a psyche in transition. If one of my core principles is that accidents are inevitable then I must also accept that relationships probably won't last. The "too much work" statement can only be made by someone who seeks permanence in a relationship, therefore the core principle isn't valid.

So that individual's emotional, spiritual and psychological well being are either forfeit or in flux. The only place where they can create permanence is (wait for it) themselves, specifically, those elements about themselves that they can both touch and not see changing on a daily basis unless they so will it.

The body becomes a canvas. There is an Italian saying, "Change my hair, change my life", meaning cut your hair short if it was long and things will change for you. Make it blond if it was brunette and things will change for you. Shave your beard if you had one and things will change for you. Tattoo if you didn't have one and things will change for you. Pierce what wasn't pierced and things will change for you.[d]

So I'm not responsible and my identity is in high flux because I'm no longer bound by any steady relationship. But our brains are designed to require both.

And in the modern world, we turn to online social networks because they provide us with identity, we can freely participate in no-cost, low-cost fair-exchanges that can be ignored or easily forgotten because so much else is going on that claims our attention, and we create relationships that have little emotional

---

[d] – How many years has there been an unspoken recognition that a girl was entering womanhood by getting her ears pierced? Cultural anthropologists recognize this as a symbolic piercing of the hymen, a statement that the maid is ready for deflowering.

meaning because they lack that key requirement for long-term relationships, the touch. Even as I write this, "the touch" has become an online commodity thanks to sites such as Tinder, Grindr and their promotion of a "hook-up" culture.[e]

The only things our brains are designed to recognize as real are those we touch, the first, most primitive sensory system and the largest sensory organ we have. We may believe photons exist and have data to prove same, we may believe god exists and have data to prove same, but the parts of our brain that deal with sensual reality only believe something exists if we can touch it, hence pull it from the ether and make it real right here, right now. Have you ever seen someone shocked or stunned by some piece of personal news or interest? Perhaps meeting someone they thought dead or missing or gone, or discovering some childhood memento that brought them great joy or pain? The first instinct is to touch, to prove it is real, to confirm its identity therefore confirm their own.

But we can't do that in online social networks. At least not yet. Our tacit (tactile) knowledge is no longer valid or recognized as valid.[165,211,300,302,365,366,532,563,620] Thank goodness for mobiles. Being able to see the person we're talking with while holding "them" in our hands is a close surrogate,[33,56] not ideal but close enough, and if that's what we have been raised with?

Like the generation coming into the workforce in the 2010s?

The fair-exchange becomes "I got what I wanted, you got what you wanted, I'm good with mine and too bad if yours isn't good for you." I'm not responsible and my identity may change as soon as this exchange is over. If I'm the one who's unsatisfied, again too bad for me, time for me to switch my identity and continue engaging in exchanges until I find one that's fair.

Of course, by this point in time, the seven million years of evolutionary wiring in my brain is so damaged by social shocks and failed exchanges that I'm a walking (dare I say it?) zombie, so numbed by modern existence that I live in a state of petite or simple social terrorism, repeatedly insulating myself from shock

---

[e] – http://www.vanityfair.com/culture/2015/08/tinder-hook-up-culture-end-of-dating

and upheaval while continually being wounded by those I reach out to.

Oy, don't it shit to be (the modern) me! Think of how all this affects the experience-expectation channel documented in *Reading Virtual Minds Volume II: Experience and Expectation*!

With so many negatives, what are the positives of digital divisivity?

Freedom from responsibility, for one. If what I need can be shared and not owned? My space requirements are less. And here there's a contradiction; My identity is no longer demonstrated by things or places, I myself become my identity. Individuals become real-world, walking, breathing, interacting digimages (we can't call them "homages") to WYSIWYG ("What You See Is What You Get" and another nod to Tinder-like sites everywhere).

We are still the sum of our experiences but now the majority of our experiences are virtual.

Oh, you shallow few. You shallow, shallow few.

Who registers disappointment when a meeting is missed or forgotten?

If no one is to blame and no one is responsible, there can be no disappointment, only acceptance and a desire to move on.

But fair-exchange must exist because it is in our core. It is the very heart of our self-definition from our first cooings and our mothers' first snuggling response. The ultimate fair-exchange is the giving of oneself in a relationship and the getting of the other person in return. Remember that we'll create community with whatever's handy (from *Reading Virtual Minds Volume I: Science and History*)? No wonder the push is on to make interfaces more and more human and life-like.

But again fair-exchange rears its head. These interfaces are based on social concepts that their immediate electronic forebears made obsolete. Talk about the pot calling the kettle black!

Unless our devices teach us an arcane form of social exchange,[150] our fair-exchanges will truly be digital ones and only with a reflection of ourselves in the machine.

Holy narcissism, Batman!

No, holy ghost in the machine, Robin, and the ghost is us.

How do we market to a population that doesn't recognize the icons of the past? How do we market to a population that doesn't recognize it's been given god-like powers (thinking of Arthur C. Clarke's famously misquoted "Any sufficiently advanced technology is indistinguishable from magic.")? Newer technologies allow us to control devices by waving our hands and flicking our wrists. We can talk and control what happens in a room. We can embed ourselves in a virtual reality that approaches StarTrek: The Next Generation™'s holodeck. The largest sense organ we have, our skin, along with our ability to learn and discover through our sense of touch,[1,226,298,389,510,620] is no longer necessary, therefore it's no longer our non-conscious demarcation between ourselves and our environment.[365,378] Yet most people who've been around babies and toddlers know that everything has to be touched. Touched, smelled, tasted, shaken (does it make a noise) and looked at. This progression isn't by accident, or if it is an accident then every child on the planet shares it. That progression climbs the ladder from the oldest sensory system, one shared with literally every other living thing on the planet, to the newest, vision, and in the order those sensory systems developed; touch, smell, taste, hearing, vision.[1,23,178,408,414,542,545]

But touch is no longer necessary. New interfaces allow us to project ourselves into our environment so the boundary of where we stop and the world begins is no longer at the surface of our flesh.[210,298,414,517,530,541] Our sense of intimacy and empathy are gone,[3,389,469,492,570] hence how we recognize kin and perform kin-selection is changed.,[159,228,328,359,389,461,560,569,618f] The new kin selection algorithm is a swipe left or right ala Tinder and Grindr.

If what one writes about the internet is invalid six months hence, what branding and logo and corporate ID will have meaning from the time it's conceived to the time it's published? Our social structure is based on our ability to record and transmit

---

[f] – And we're not even getting close to what happens to our immune systems if we're somaesthetic. We lose proprioception and related somatic senses, we no longer recognize when our skin is damaged. We become lepers without the benefit of leprosy.

past knowledge forward, eliminating the need for rediscovery. Past mistakes need not be repeated with each new generation.

But if what we record and transmit is only valid during the moment of transmission (ie, the moment of exchange)?

We come back to one of the questions asked in *Reading Virtual Minds Volume II: Experience and Expectation*'s *Author's Foreword*[g]: How do you market to gods?

Easy, don't worry about six months out. Don't worry about six days out. Satisfy them now, in the moment, and be happy you did.

Nobody wants to suffer the wrath of the gods.

And the majority of gods weren't especially kind to mortals.

> **Take-Away #21 – The lifecycle of a device interface is determined by most used features across most often users. when frequent users stop using, redesign asap**

---

[g] – I told you to buy copies and read them, didn't I?

I value my garden more for being full of blackbirds than of cherries, and very frankly give them fruit for their song.
– Joseph Addison

7 - Fair-Exchange, Floor-to-Ceiling Studies and Concept Price

Floor-to-Ceiling studies deal with concepts of value as they apply to attainable goals. Normally the value of something is fixed by the investigators and becomes the ceiling, as in "this is what the market will bear". The floor depends on the study's subjects and deals with their perception of their ability to reach the ceiling, i.e., pay the market value for the goods or service. The function of floor-to-ceiling studies is to determine the effort a group or individual will apply to reach the ceiling. These studies become fascinating for two primary reasons. One, they are the role model for negotiations. Two, according to basic economic theory human beings always work harder to avoid losing what they already have rather than to acquire more because loss is always more devastating than the potential for gain is motivating.

Say you're a middle-income individual and in the market for a car. Chances are you're not going to begin your car search with Lamborghinis or Testarosas. The ceiling is too high and the effort to go from your floor to their ceiling is too great. Likewise, you're pretty sure that the people selling such cars wouldn't be able to make financing affordable to you so the ceiling, in your mind, is fairly well fixed (we're ignoring the house mortgage debacle of 2007-2009[a]).

But what if the car is a simple economy car. The distance from the floor to the ceiling is much less and definitely traversable. But there are two forces in this system not often recognized as part of the system. One is the ability of the seller to change the ceiling and second is the size of the market. Too large a market and the ceiling has difficulty fluctuating. This is obvious to anyone who's gone price shopping on the internet for a major brand. The large market translates into broad demand which equates to the ceiling – or perceived market value – being fairly stable during the lifetime of the market. But decrease the market

---

[a] – https://en.wikipedia.org/wiki/Subprime_mortgage_crisis

size enough and the seller can modify the ceiling within certain limits. This was also obvious to anyone wanting to purchase an SUV when gas prices climbed on a daily basis during the early 2010s.

Most often the ceiling is fixed for a product and the floor varies according to the abilities of the buyer to pay. The price of milk is the price of milk is the price of milk, but to the low-income family of five milk is expensive and may even fall into the luxury category. This gets into the area of *concept price*.[68,71,420]

Concept price plays a large part in personal financial decision making and is the neuroeconomic form of opportunity cost. Imagine a consumer going shopping for some item. When the cost of that item is so low that it essentially doesn't affect the consumer's life – when they don't have to plan how to pay for the item or how to afford other necessary items because the desired item creates some real or imagined financial challenge or hardship – the concept price is low to insignificant. For most consumers, a quart of milk has an insignificant concept price.

Now let's make that item a mid-price car such as a Ford or Chrysler. A middle-income consumer has to plan for that purchase, has to decide what might be given up in order to make the payments. The concept price is high; What happens if the job is lost or there's a family emergency? But the concept price of the same vehicle is not so high for an upper-income consumer. A $20k car purchased by a $250k/year income consumer might be qualified as an impulse purchase.

Now let's return to the high-end car purchase for a middle-income earner and let's make it reasonable, say a low-end Porsche. The concept price goes through the roof; Do they buy the car or put their kid through school? Usually other decision makers get involved as concept price goes up (regardless of income level) and keeping those decision makers out of the loop can cause hardship in itself.

A general rule is that price is secondary except when it hits against some form of concept price.

To the high-income family of two, milk is just something you get. Getting back to buying a Lamborghini, the market is very small and most buyers don't enter the market without a high degree of confidence in their ability to reach the ceiling and afford the car. Here the distance from floor to ceiling is also small but the seller's ability to modify the ceiling is fixed by the small market size. In either case, a seller who arbitrarily increases or decreases the ceiling destroys the market. The ability of the seller to manipulate the ceiling within certain parameters is, in the vernacular, "wiggle room". An equation (I know, you just couldn't wait for me to throw in an equation) which states this takes the form:

$$C = W + F \ || \ \lim_{(F \to C)} \Delta W = 0$$

The above is read as "The Ceiling value of an item equals the seller's Wiggle room + the buyer's Floor such that as the buyer's ability to pay approaches the seller's price there's less and less wiggle room in the negotiation."

The wiggle room, though, is where fair-exchange takes place. Way back in the beginning of this book we talked about fair-exchanges taking place in the heart long before the value of something was accepted in the mind. The car dealer who says "I'll throw in this and this and this" is attempting to convince the buyer a fair-exchange is taking place. The ceiling or market value of the car may be US$25,000 but the buyer's floor is US$19,500. The seller is negotiating, wiggling if you will, a higher fair-exchange value for the same dollar amount, essentially saying "I'll give you a US$30,000 car for only US$25,000" in the hopes that the buyer will perceive the increased value as a fair-exchange for the original US$25,000 market value of the car.

Take-Away #22 – Make sure what you value and what your audience/client/user/visitor values are identical before attempting to wiggle

A common flaw in "value" based negotiations is recognizing what's valuable in different value systems (we're back to our Amerinds and Colonials again), and we're now able to recognize that fair-exchange is a social function and not a market function. Personal and business deals are often quashed only because one or the other party felt a fair-exchange didn't take place even though everyone agreed to the elements of the exchange. This is often because the social function of a fair-exchange derives from shared signs and symbols between the parties involved. The investor feels the inventor didn't show adequate respect so decides not to invest in the invention. The inventor feels the investor didn't appreciate the time and effort that went into the invention so decides to look elsewhere. Both believe the other a fool when all that really happened was that necessary signs weren't exchanged. This exchange of signs also takes place in the wiggle room, and often the amount of wiggling that goes on approaches infinity the closer and closer the floor approaches the ceiling. This becomes

$$\lim_{(F \to C)} (C - F) = \lim_{(W \to \infty)} \Delta F$$

and is read as "The closer the ceiling and floor values become the more wiggling is done as the floor value changes."

What fascinates me as a researcher is that the real cost of effort (as calculated over the lifetime of the buyer) to reach the ceiling is the same regardless of where the buyer's floor starts.

Wiggle room and how it's applied plays heavily in the next chapter, where ceiling and floor are fixed by the nature of online transactions.

If you're not paying for it, you're not the customer.
You're the product being sold.
- Andrew Lewis

8 - The New Cost of Information

Earlier in this book I mentioned individuals who have more than one email account and that the criteria for which email account you're given depends on what level of access the holder of the account wishes to grant you. This plethora of email accounts equates to the ability to create and destroy identities and the social networks they dwell in with far greater fluidity than ever before in the history of humanity.

What it also demonstrates is information inflation – you have to give more to get the same quality of information you could get before for less. This is where the floor-to-ceiling and wiggle room are all but destroyed thanks to the anonymity of the web. Let's go back to the car buyer metaphor to explain.

John is a low-income father with big dreams. He can go to a car buying site and put together an order for a car far beyond any ceiling he could reasonably reach. Never-the-less, he is capable of doing it, even to the point of creating an identity which supports his fantasy solely for the purpose of playing his game. This surrogate self has a completely different personal access floor from which to operate. The criminal aspect of this is known as identity theft. John takes on an existing identity and makes use of its floor to achieve a desired ceiling. When sufficient numbers of people fail to understand their personal financial ceilings and the market chooses to ignore the concept, you're back to the previously mentioned US home mortgage crisis of 2007 and beyond.

Fortunately, a more common example of the new cost of information is our simple case of an individual with multiple email addresses, each with a different floor and ceiling set by the individual who creates them. But in this case, it is the online business which comes in at some unknown floor (to them) and must achieve some unknown ceiling (again to them). Long ago in internet time, a website could ask for some fairly high quality information before giving out a paper or allowing a download. Now not so much so. Sites that set their ceiling too high run the risk of not getting any business at all. So where is the wiggle room?

The wiggle room comes in primarily two forms. The first is the use of different information delivery technologies. Do you want to take part in a webinar? Then the quality of information you exchange for that privilege must necessarily be higher that the quality of information you exchange to download a whitepaper or case study. In all cases the business's goal is to get quality information from you with which to touch you again. Go to a site with free downloads often enough or download some threshold in a single session and *zing!* a popup or alert box or some such activates to either stop you, make you pay or otherwise get your attention (identity information).

Likewise and in all cases, your goal is to provide the lowest quality information possible to prevent the business from being able to touch you unless you wish it. The problem with this model is that there is an assumption of value at the time of the exchange which might not be met when delivered and *oops!* the business loses a potential client. We're now asking, "Who's in control of the exchange?" and answering that makes all the axes vibrate.

The second form of wiggle room makes use of the fair-exchange model as it applies to social networks and viral dynamics and was first described in *Reading Virtual Minds Volume II: Experience and Expectation* section 7.C – Removing Barriers to Entry and Qualification Upon Re-Entry. Allow the user to take part in some online activity with no information cost involved. The exchange, if you wish to define it as such, is the entry in your weblogs of the visitor's activity. The fair-exchange is different. The visitor gave you nothing and you gave them nothing (if whatever they got had real value you wouldn't be giving it away). What the visitor got is your trust that, if they found whatever they got worthwhile, they'd return to let you know such. What you got is a viral messenger propagating your message in a social network you normally couldn't touch. It's best to accept the social network's reach regardless of whatever message is propagated. Much like the adage "There's no such thing as bad publicity", in an age where digital divisivity allows everyone's ego to guide some ship for some finite period of time, trust becomes a marketable commodity.

As a species, humans are designed to pay more attention to negative information than positive because negative information tended to have survival value associated with it. There is more survival value associated with "Thalia doesn't know how to cure snakebite" than "Lem is the best person to cure snakebite" because I can go to lots of people if Lem isn't around but if it's a choice between Thalia and one other person, I definitely need to stay away from Thalia. Amazon and other etailers make use of this in their recommendations (note that we're discussing etailers, not individuals. Nobody wants a negative review on LinkedIn but people can post negative reviews of businesses anywhere they like. Facebook's move to add a "DisLike" button is a nod to this[a]. Reddit's downvote has been offering this concept for quite a while...in internet time). Etailers and others have learned that lots of positive reviews drive down sales. Put one or two negative reviews into the mix and sales climb. The business equivalent of this is wanting to know business failures rather than successes because knowing what to avoid helps you better define your path to your goal than just knowing someone else's success path without understanding the challenges they had along the way.

There are some who claim that the "no information cost" model is flawed. I offer that it isn't flawed but that it works on a time-scale which might be inappropriate for some applications. NextStage conducted an experiment to determine the efficacy of the latter method on several websites. In all cases, exchanges skyrocketed. Where there might have been ten exchanges per month there were now several hundred per week. Further, the material websites offered in the exchanges started appearing on other websites and in other venues, all with pointers back to the originating sites. Traffic increased and business soon followed. In

---

[a] – http://www.techtimes.com/articles/85066/20150920/facebook-social-media-mark-zuckerberg-like-dislike.htm

this model, even visitors who don't exchange fairly (harking back to social theorists' and ethologists' concepts of "free-riders"[38,51, 166,257,323,360,433,494,560] and "cheaters"[32,38,51,63,166,236,257,323, 345,360,419,433,460,494,496,560]) pass the viral information on and thus the business's goal is achieved. Cheaters and free-riders become superior cooperators[193,215,291,431,438,478,502,526,528,533,557,588] due to the nature of the exchange. When a sufficiently large group engages in a fair-exchange but does not exchange fairly, new social orders and individuals evolve. In this case, a single mutation can save, change or alter an industry depending on the industry's adaptability, vulnerability and acceptance factors.

The only real currency is that of a peculiar morality not easily found in the modern world - to exchange one's best efforts for the best efforts of another.

9 - Getting as Good as You Give

Let's consider fair-exchange in immediately recognizable terms. Say you're an etailer who wants to increase your audience/customer base. The traditional "give as good as you get" model places you and your audience in conflict, both sides ever-watchful that they don't reveal more than they need to get what they want. The traditional model paves the way for deceptive practices on both sides (consumers with junk email accounts, bogus phone numbers, et cetera, and etailers offering material that is more marketing hype than informational content).

You, an honorable etailer, want to increase your audience/customer base by asking visitors for their email address.

But what do you offer in return?

Does the visitor perceive your offer as equal in value to their email address? if so, why do so many people have junk email addresses?

Fair-exchange occurs when individuals share an understanding of what is being given and what is being received. The shared understanding might be that they've just bettered each other. The Amerinds thought they made out on the deal and so did the Colonists. Because both felt themselves successful in the exchange, trust was created that made further exchanges possible. Note: the Amerinds weren't necessarily trusting the Colonists and the Colonists weren't necessarily trusting the Amerinds, however each trusted themselves that they got what they wanted and gave up what they were willing to give up; the Amerinds trusted the Colonists to trade valuable goods for something with no real value and vice versa.

Sometimes an agent is required to facilitate fair-exchanges in the marketplace and a requirement of the agent is that this agent is able to communicate equally and evenly to all parties involved with favoritism to none. A mid-level manager who has no ability other than to accurately exchange information between subordinates and superiors has great value simply because of that skill. My anecdote about the NextStage investor communicating to me with signs and signals I could understand and also being able to facilitate exchanges in the business world was an example of this. The moment favoritism is revealed so is the agent and any hope for a fair-exchange is gone.

Fair-exchange also occurs in apparently altruistic situations. The individual performing the altruistic act increases their social value, worth and collateral within their community – their own rationale might be that they simply feel good by performing the altruistic deed – and quite possibly gains access to different social networks by their act. Gaining social value, worth and access to if not mobility in different social networks is a key motivator in online altruistic acts.

The reason social value, worth and currency in different social networks is granted (especially due to online altruistic acts) is because such acts promote trust and trust is a key component of fair-exchanges.

Trust is created in fair-exchanges via negotiations and the negotiations have to use signs and symbols in which all parties recognize a common meaning. But it isn't easy to know that all parties recognize a common meaning in online transactions, therefore trust is assigned to unknown parties via the use of different identities created for just such a purpose[a].

However, the cost of information on the web is often too high for any fair-exchange to take place and the result is sometimes wish-based behavior if not outright unlawful behavior. A solution for businesses is to follow the Amerind-Colonists model; create a fair-exchange in which the business supplies something the prospect values in exchange for the prospect telling other

---

[a] – At the time of this writing, PayPal and Craigslist are examples of a trusted exchange agents. The fair-exchange between buyer and seller must still take place, PayPal and Craigslist only serve to guarantee that, should one or the other party decide no fair-exchange took place, the exchange reverts to its original state. Note that this means PayPal, Craigslist, etc., ensure they will invoke fair-exchanges with both buyer and seller if buyer and seller believe no fair-exchange has taken place in their negotiations. Credit card companies do a weak form of this, this weakness is exploited and people complain about credit card rates, additional fees, unsatisfactory dispute resolutions, etc., and all are examples of non-fair-exchanges.

prospects and self-qualifying. The fair-exchange in this situation
is first between the business and the viral environment of the
web via an altruistic act with the goal of the business increasing
its social value and gaining access to new social networks. Then,
because trust has been established, other fair-exchanges will
occur between the business and the prospects themselves.

Let me again bring our focus to online behaviors and more
specifically to ET and its purpose of learning how people
communicate online. ET, in many situations, is acting as an agent
and facilitating communication between the site visitor and the
business owning the site. As in my example with NextStage
Global's CEO, it is able to communicate with both parties without
showing partiality to either and treating both fairly, honestly and
openly.

How does ET do this? First, ET doesn't require the visitor to
submit any information or answer any forms. ET does all the
monitoring and makes decisions based on observations its
performed over time with all visitors to all sites it monitors. What
visitors have done and how the current visitor is behaving in
respect to all its known and is learning is part of its analysis and
decision process. This is not to suggest that ET doesn't ask
questions or get answers to them, it's just that ET asks questions
and gets answers in ways that most people aren't used to. A fair-
exchange is taking place, it's simply unrecognizable as such.

ET actually spends most of its interaction time with
individuals first initiating then maintaining a one-to-one
conversation. The conversation (at present, anyway) – the
information exchange – is done this way; ET asks a question by
presenting the individual with some information. The individual
answers by the way they interact with that information. Based on
the individual's answer, ET asks another question via another or
modified information presentation. The individual's interaction is
their next answer, so on and so forth. Based on the individual's
answers, ET's questions become increasingly specific to the
individual's needs. The fair-exchange is the individual's trust in
exchange for information increasingly utilizing the signs and
symbols that individual is most comfortable with.

So what has ET learned about creating fair-exchanges in cyberspace? We start with an example of a reasonable fair-exchange graphed and shown in figure 9.1 on page 124. Figure 9.1 is an aggregate of all visitors to all sites during a given time period.

ET records a near perfect fair-exchange when the shapes of the visitor (green/top) and site (red/bottom) lines are identical and the peaks are close to each other. A flat or near flat visitor (green) line indicates the visitor isn't even aware an exchange is taking place. The vertical axis measures differences in subjective values and are calculated from the visitor's perspective. The horizontal axis is correlated to the set {-1, 0, +1} representing {no exchange, exchange, no exchange} with |-1| = |+1|. In a truly good fair-exchange situation the lines have the same shape and are separated by a small fixed value throughout.[b] Experience has demonstrated that the site owner usually believes they're giving away more than they're getting and this comes through in the design.

The difference between the heights of the left end of the lines indicates that the visitor believes either they or the site isn't giving enough in return for whatever is being requested, ie, the exchange is not fair. Likewise, the right end of the lines indicates that the visitor believes either they or the site isn't getting enough in return for whatever was requested and again the exchange isn't fair. The above chart and the ones following can be thought of as a graphical representation of the fair-exchange multidimensional balance shown on page 44. The apex of the visitor and site lines is the balance point of the figure and the lines themselves are the arms of the balance.

---

[b] – Some readers have been challenged by ET's charts because ET's charts rarely show numerical values. The reason ET's charts rarely show exacting numerical values is because very often the values are irrelevant and the shapes presented are extremely relevant. These charts are examples of the latter. The numbers themselves don't have much meaning, the shapes presented by the lines, their proximity, when they peak and how, etc., are all highly relevant to determining if a Fair-Exchange is taking place.

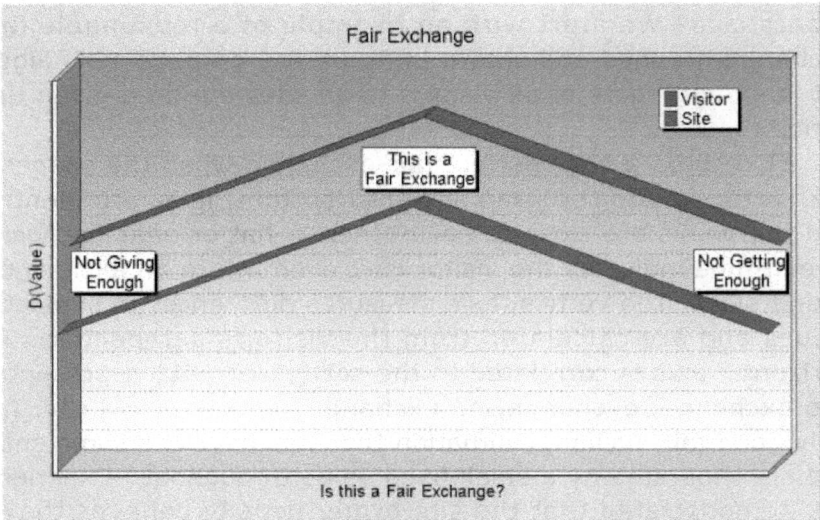

9.1 - This is an example of a Good Fair-Exchange

Now let's consider some actual exchanges ET has recorded and describe the circumstances which caused them. First, let's look at the graph of an exchange that won't take place (figure 9.2 on page 124).

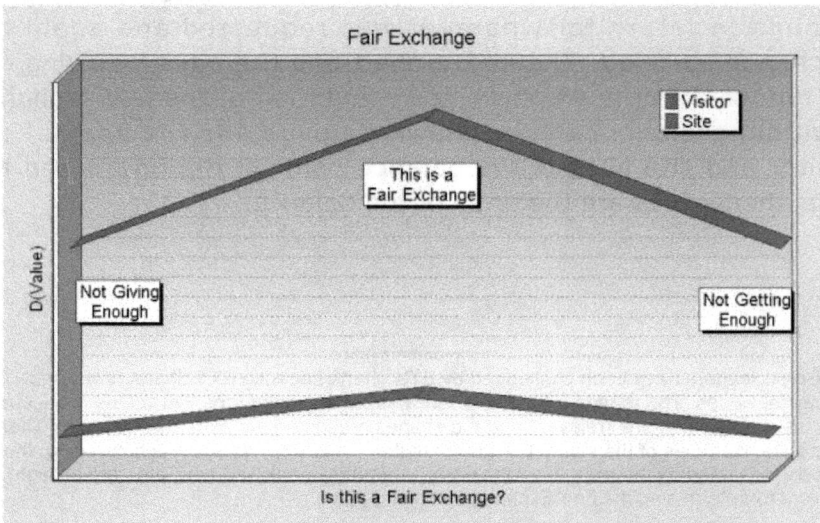

9.2 - This exchange won't take place

Figure 9.2 is a fair-exchange chart from mid-2001 that's based on interactions for the page shown in figure 9.3 (page 125). A client site required visitors to fill in about a page of contact information (including a text box wherein prospects described their reason for requesting the material) prior to downloading a product brochure. The distance between the end points of the visitor (green/top) and site (red/bottom) lines indicate that visitors believed the site wasn't giving enough nor were they getting enough for the information required. The differences in the angles of the two lines (the site (red/bottom) line is flatter than the visitor (green/top) line) indicate that visitors felt the amount of effort involved was also excessive when matched to the materials received.

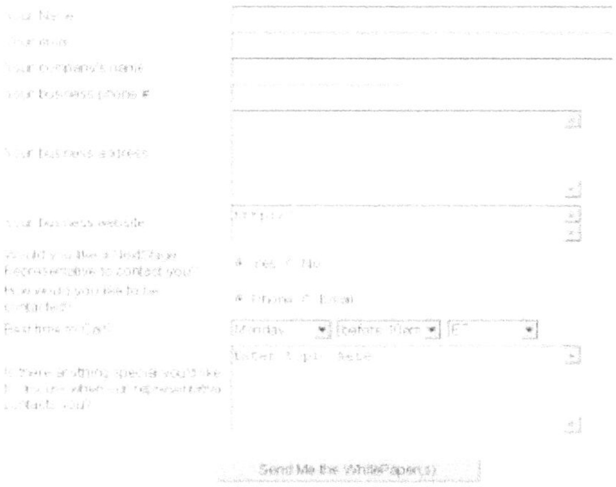

Figure 9.3 - Even in 2001, visitors considered the amount of information requested to receive a whitepaper to be an unfair-exchange

Next we look at a fair-exchange chart from the same client site two months later, this time with no requirement for download whatsoever (figures 9.4-5 on pages 126-127). The visitor (green/top) line is above the site (red/bottom) line on the left and below it on the right. This is an example of visitor believing the exchange isn't fair because they (visitors) aren't giving enough. The result was distrust of the site. Something had to be given for value to be received, or what was being received had no value, therefore the game shouldn't be played.

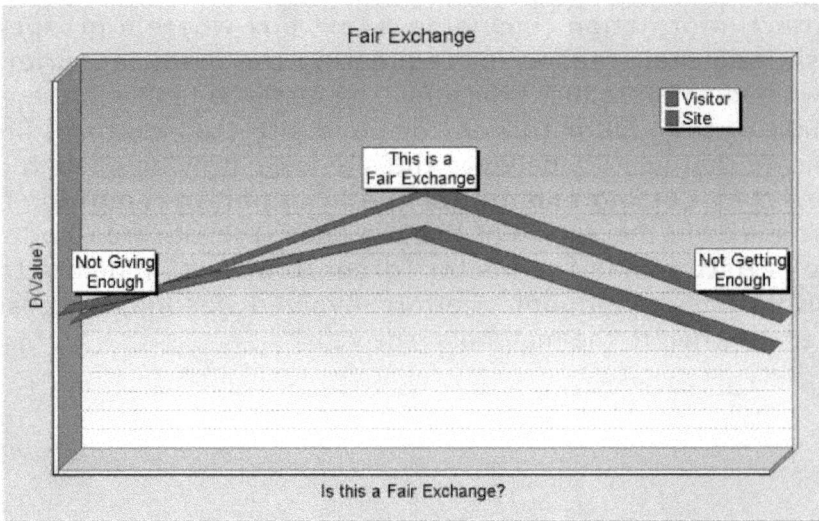

9.4 - The visitor beleives they aren't giving enough

The next modification the client made was three months later. Visitors were asked to fill in name, email address, company position, company name, address and phone number fields in return for a sample product shipment (figure 9.6 on page 127). What is important about this case was that visitors didn't receive any immediate value for the information they presented. Filling in the required fields got them to a "Thank You" page but nothing more. Visitors didn't believe the exchange was fair because they provided value for no immediate return, i.e., they weren't getting enough for what they were giving *at the moment the information was exchanged*.

The final chart (figure 9.7 on page 128) shows the results of a single site modification to the above. After the visitor filled in the required information a shipment receipt was included on the "Thank You" page with an invitation to print the receipt out. The receipt also included the expected number of days involved in shipping. The closeness of the lines and similar angles indicate that the visitor was satisfied with the exchange. The site (red) line's peak being just above the visitor's (green) peak indicates the visitor thought the exchange was almost one-for-one and literally, each party involved gave as good as they got.

1-2-3 for defining your Visitor Action Metric

Defining your VAM is as easy as 1.2.3. Here's all you need to do:

1) Create a logical path from your home or landing page to the conversion metric page
2) Create an emotional path from your home or landing page to the conversion metric page (it's fairly well documented that most people make decisions based on emotion first then look for logical reasons for them)
3) Make sure that each page on your logical path has a VAM that satisfies the corresponding element on the emotional path. Place a clear, concise and logical decision point at the end of the VAM. Ask yourself: Are visitors taking the turn in the road you want them to take? If not, there is no conversion event and you need to adjust your VAM.

Remember that each successful turn in the road is a conversion event in the visitor's mind. If you know how to lead, they will follow.

Did you find this whitepaper helpful?
Would you like to read other whitepapers in this series?

Please go to www.kayesology.com for more papers in this series, and thanks.

Figure 9.5 - Barriers to entry are removed and the exchange is fair...or at least fairer than it was

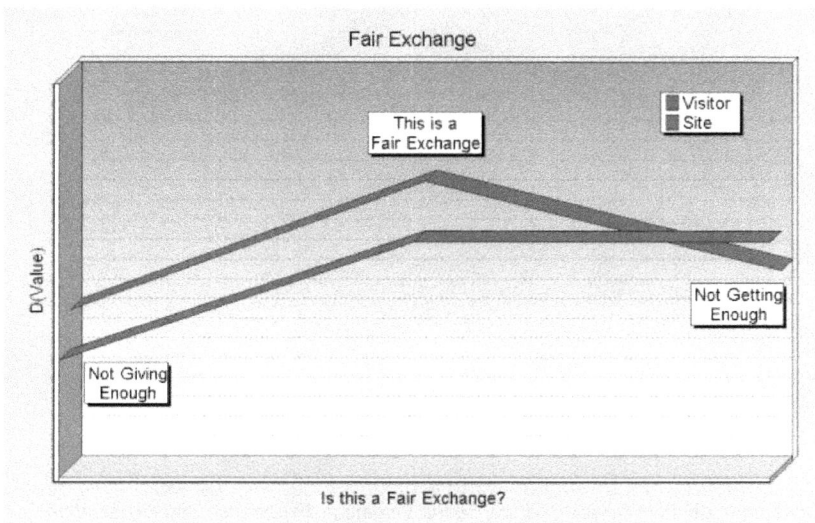

9.6 - Visitors didn't believe they were receiving enough in the exchange

In the examples above two factors need to be brought forward. These examples cover about a year's time from mid-2001 to mid-2002. Times have changed since then and the cost of information has risen dramatically since then. Likewise, newer technologies allow for increased wiggle room when sites and visitors engage in fair-exchanges. NextStage's use of qualification upon re-entry and viral methodologies[c] – things which were unheard of back in 2001-2 – increased conversions by some 300%, not to mention increasing recognition and trust in social networks in which client sites previously didn't engage. As one individual commented, "No one called me and said, 'I heard your podcast, we're interested.' But lots of people remarked on it and I did get new business plus now I know the podcaster and he knows everyone...". The fair-exchange occurred because of a seemingly altruistic event which lead to an increase in social worth and access to previously unknown markets and networks, which came from increased trust, which led to business. Kind of the reverse of "For the lack of a nail..."

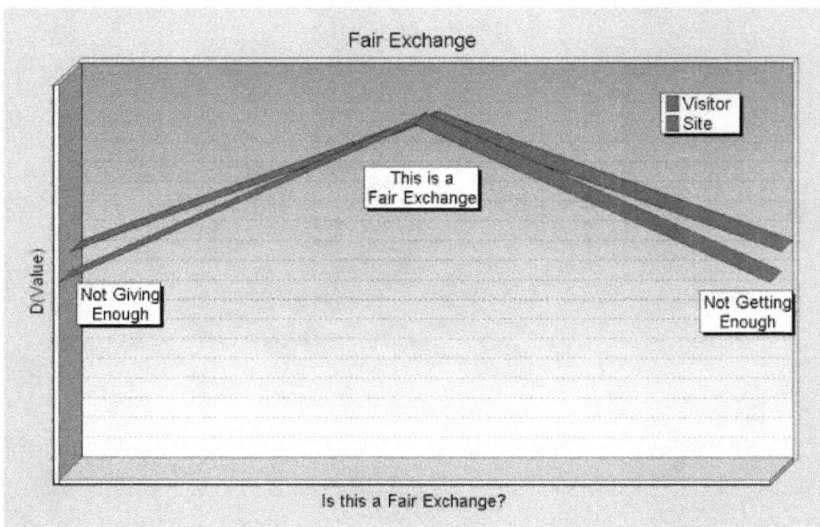

9.7 - This is a near perfect exchange

---

[c] – Covered in detail in *Reading Virtual Minds Volume II: Experience and Expectation* (http://nlb.pub/RVMV21st) and why haven't you ordered a copy yet?

As I write this in late Summer of 2016, companies have the ability to monitor wiggle room and provide standards with predefined wiggles built in. It's now possible for etailers to offer near instantaneous phone contact or chat if a visitor requests it. Of course, the price – the information-exchange – of fulfilling this request involves the visitor previously providing some high value information before hand. For example, the visitor may already be a client who's provided both contact information and coin of the realm, been involved in previous, less involved exchanges, demonstrated an ability for proaction with the etailer rather than simple reaction and so on. Some etailers offer personal and guaranteed one-on-one service if the visitor requests it (the "requests it" is crucial because the less it is requested the higher the visitor's value) and such sites cater to visitors with recognized high-potential value right out of the box.

The only way such exchanges are possible is because the internet has become the new British Empire. At one point in time the sun never set on the British Empire. Now the sun never sets on the internet and the cost of information-exchange has suffered for it.

Take-Away #23 – Design to the lowest common denominator to get the largest possible audience. But beware, the largest possible audience will get you the lowest number of conversions as a percentage of that audience[d]

---

[d] – NextStage's advice to a Philadelphia based client who was getting 10k hits/month and only 1-2 conversions/month.

The secret to creativity is knowing how to hide your sources. - Albert Einstein

Further Readings

1. Ackerley, R., Backlund Wasling, H., Liljencrantz, J., Olausson, H., Johnson, R. D., & Wessberg, J. (2014, 19 Feb). Human C-Tactile Afferents Are Tuned to the Temperature of a Skin-Stroking Caress. *The Journal of Neuroscience, 34*(8), 2879–2883. (Http://www.jneurosci.org/content/34/8/2879.full.pdf+html)
2. Ackerley, R., Wild, K., & Makin, A. (2008, 3 Sep). Cognitive Influences on the Generation of Eye Movements. *The Journal of Neuroscience, 28*(36), 8863–8864. (Http://www.jneurosci.org/content/28/36/8863.full.pdf+html)
3. Ackerman, J. M., Nocera, C. C., & Bargh, J. A. (2010, 25 Jun). Incidental Haptic Sensations Influence Social Judgments and Decisions. *Science, 328*(5986), 1712–1715. (Http://www.sciencemag.org/content/328/5986/1712.full.pdf)
4. Ackerman, J. M., Shapiro, J. R., Neuberg, S. L., Kenrick, D. T., Becker, D. V., Griskevicius, V., et al. (2006, 1 Oct). They All Look the Same to Me (Unless They're Angry). *Psychological Science, 17*(10), 836–840. (Http://www.nature.com/nature/journal/v439/n7072/pdf/nature04340.pdf)
5. Acquisti, A., Brandimarte, L., & Loewenstein, G. (2015, 30 Jan). Privacy and human behavior in the age of information. *Science, 347*(6221), 509–514. (Http://www.sciencemag.org/content/347/6221/509.full.pdf)
6. Adam J. Rubenstein. (2005, Oct). Variation in Perceived Attractiveness. *Psychological Science, 16*(10), 759–762. (Http://www3.interscience.wiley.com/cgi-bin/fulltext/118661656/PDFSTART)
7. Adam, S., Mulye, R., Deans, & Palihawadana, D. (2001). A Three Country Comparison of Internet Marketing. Australian and New Zealand Marketing Academy Conference. Massey University, Auckland, NZ. (Http://www.stewartadam.com/publications/adam_mulye_deans_ANZMAC_2001.pdf)

8. Adam, S., & Shaw, R. (2001). Experiential Dimensions in Internet Marketing: An Exploratory Investigation. Australian and New Zealand Marketing Academy Conference. Massey University, Auckland, NZ. (Http://www.stewartadam.com/publications/adam_shaw_ANZMAC_2001.pdf)

9. Adams, R. B., Jr., Gordon, H. L., Baird, A. A., Ambady, N., & Kleck, R. E. (2003, 6 Jun). Effects of Gaze on Amygdala Sensitivity to Anger and Fear Faces. *Science, 300*(5625).

10. Adolf Tobeña. (2009). Lethal Altruists : Itineraries along the Dark Outskirts of Moralistic Prosociality. *Annals of the New York Academy of Sciences, 1167*(Values, Empathy, and Fairness across Social Barriers), 5–15. (Http://www3.interscience.wiley.com/cgi-bin/fulltext/122466378/PDFSTART)

11. Aharon, I., Etcoff, N., Ariely, D., Chabris, C. F., O'Connor, E., & Breiter, H. C. (2001, 8 Nov). Beautiful Faces Have Variable Reward Value: FMRI and Behavioral Evidence. *Neuron, 32*(3), 537–551. (Http://download.cell.com/neuron/pdf/PIIS0896627301004913.pdf)

12. Almays, I., Cappelen, A. W., SÃ¸rensen, E. Ã., & Tungodden, B. (2010, 28 May). Fairness and the Development of Inequality Acceptance. *Science, 328*(5982), 1176–1178. (Http://www.sciencemag.org/content/328/5982/1176.full.pdf)

13. Almeida, J., Mahon, B. Z., & Caramazza, A. (2010, 1 Jun). The Role of the Dorsal Visual Processing Stream in Tool Identification. *Psychological Science, 21*(6), 772–778. (Http://pss.sagepub.com/content/21/6/772.full.pdf+html)

14. Anderson, B. A., Laurent, P. A., & Yantis, S. (2013, 11 Jun). Reward predictions bias attentional selection. *Frontiers in Human Neuroscience, 7.* (Http://www.frontiersin.org/Journal/DownloadFile.ashx?pdf=1&FileId=256363&articleId=50195&Version=1&ContentTypeId=21&FileName=fnhum-07-00262.pdf)

15. Anderson, C. A., & Bushman, B. J. (2002, 29 Mar). The Effects of Media Violence on Society. *Science, 295*(5564), 2377–

2379.
(Http://www.sciencemag.org/cgi/reprint/sci;295/5564/2377.pdf)
16. Andrew J. Mashburn, L. M. J., Jason T. Downer. (2009). Peer
Effects on Children's Language Achievement During Pre-
Kindergarten. *Child Development, 80*(3), 686–702.
17. Arcadi Navarro. (2009). Genoeconomics: Promises and
Caveats for a New Field. *Annals of the New York Academy of
Sciences, 1167*(Values, Empathy, and Fairness across Social
Barriers), 57–65. (Http://www3.interscience.wiley.com/cgi-
bin/fulltext/122466381/PDFSTART)
18. Arthur, R., & Diamond, J. (2011, 18 Nov). Understanding
Tribal Fates. *Science, 334*(6058), 911–912.
(Http://www.sciencemag.org/content/334/6058/911.full.pdf)
19. Arzy, S., Seeck, M., Ortigue, S., Spinelli, L., Blanke, & Olaf.
(2006, 21 Sept). Induction of an illusory shadow person.
Nature, 433.
20. Awofeso, N., & Green, S. (2001, Oct). Numismatics:
Australian two-dollar coin, and Aboriginal Identity. *Journal of
Mundane Behavior, 2*(3), 345–353.
21. Baglione, V., Canestrari, D., Marcos, J. M., & Ekman, J.
(2003, 20 Jun). Kin Selection in Cooperative Alliances of Carrion
Crows. *Science, 300*(5627), 1947–1949.
(Http://www.sciencemag.org/cgi/reprint/sci;300/5627/1947.pdf)
22. Bainbridge, W. S. (2003, 5 Dec). Privacy and Property on the
Net: Research Questions. *Science, 302*(5651), 1686–1687.
(Http://www.sciencemag.org/cgi/reprint/302/5651/1686.pdf)
23. Bakalar, N. (2012, 21 Jun). Partners in flavour.
Nature, 486(7403), S4-S5.
(Http://www.nature.com/nature/journal/v486/n7403_supp/pdf/4
86S4a.pdf)
24. Ballard, T., & Blaine, A. (2011). User search-limiting behavior
in online catalogs: Comparing classic catalog use to search
behavior in next-generation catalogs. *New Library World, 112*(s
5–6), 261–273.
25. Barik, J., Marti, F., Morel, C., Fernandez, S. P., Lanteri, C.,
Godeheu, G., et al. (2013, 18 Jan). Chronic Stress Triggers Social
Aversion via Glucocorticoid Receptor in Dopaminoceptive

Neurons. *Science, 339*(6117), 332–335.
(Http://www.sciencemag.org/content/339/6117/332.full.pdf)
26. Barnes, N. G., & Lescault, A. M. (2014). *Millennials Drive Social Commerce: Turning Their Likes, Follows or Pins Into a Sale.* UMass Dartmouth: Center for Marketing Research.
27. Basu, S., Dickhaut, J., Hecht, G., Towry, K., & Waymire, G. (2009, 27 Jan). Recordkeeping alters economic history by promoting reciprocity. *Proceedings of the National Academy of Sciences, 106*(4), 1009–1014.
(Http://www.pnas.org/content/106/4/1009.full.pdf+html)
28. Beardsley, E. (2015, 2 Jan). *Why Buy When You Can Borrow? App Connects People And Stuff.* NPR.
(Http://www.npr.org/blogs/alltechconsidered/2015/01/02/37418
4584/why-buy-when-you-can-borrow-app-connects-people-and-stuff)
29. Bekoff, M., & Allen, C. (1998). Intentional communication and social play: How and why animals negotiate and agree to play. In M. Bekoff & J. Byers (Eds.), *Animal Play: Evolutionary, Comparative, and Ecological Perspectives.* Cambridge and New York: Cambridge University Press.
30. Bekoff, M. (2001). Social play behaviour. Cooperation, fairness, trust, and the evolution of morality. *Journal of Consciousness Studies, 8*(2), 81–90.
31. Bekoff, M. (2002, 19 Sep). Animal reflections.
Nature, 419(6904), 255–255.
(Http://www.nature.com/nature/journal/v419/n6904/pdf/419255
a.pdf)
32. Bell, R., & Buchner, A. (2009). Enhanced source memory for names of cheaters. *Evolutionary Psychology, 7*(2), 317–330.
(Http://www.epjournal.net/filestore/ep07317330.pdf)
33. Ben Harush, O. (2007). Reflections on women using mobile phones. In M. (. Albion & P. (. Collins, *Education, Employment, and Everything: The triple layers of a woman's life.* University of Southern Queensland, Toowoomba, Queensland, Australia: IWC (International Women's Conference) 2007.

34. Berens, B. (1998). Shakespearean Contingencies: Repertory Allusion and the Birth of Mass Culture. Berkeley: University of California.

35. Bernhard, H., Fischbacher, U., & Fehr, E. (2006, 24 Aug). Parochial altruism in humans. *Nature, 442*(7105), 912–915. (Http://www.nature.com/nature/journal/v442/n7105/pdf/nature04981.pdf)

36. Berns, G. S., & Moore, S. E. (2012, Jan). A neural predictor of cultural popularity. *Journal of Consumer Psychology, 22*(1), 154–160. (Http://www.sciencedirect.com/science/article/pii/S1057740811000532)

37. Bernstein, M. J., Sacco, D. F., Brown, C. M., Young, S. G., & Claypool, H. M. (2010). A preference for genuine smiles following social exclusion. *Journal of Experimental Social Psychology, 46*(1), 196–199. (Http://www.sciencedirect.com/science?_ob=MImg&_imagekey=B6WJB-4X3N47F-1-7&_cdi=6874&_user=10&_pii=S0022103109002133&_origin=search&_coverDate=01%2F31%2F2010&_sk=999539998&view=c&wchp=dGLbVzb-zSkWA&md5=456c81b5fb9adb79272420ab3ffdf933&ie=/sdarticle.pdf)

38. Beverland, M., & Lindgreen, A. (2007). Relationships or Transactions? Marketing Practice in the Wine Trade. Monash University; Université catholique de Louvain.

39. Bewley, T. (2003, 13 Mar). Fair's fair. *Nature, 422*(6928), 125–126. (Http://www.nature.com/nature/journal/v422/n6928/pdf/422125b.pdf)

40. Bicknell, J. (2007). Explaining Strong Emotional Responses to Music. *Journal of Consciousness Studies, 14*(12), 5–23.

41. Biederman, I., Yue, X., & Davidoff, J. (2009, 1 Dec). Representation of Shape in Individuals From a Culture With Minimal Exposure to Regular, Simple Artifacts: Sensitivity to Nonaccidental Versus Metric Properties. *Psychological*

Science, 20(12), 1437–1442.
(Http://pss.sagepub.com/content/20/12/1437.full.pdf+html)
42. Blood, A. J., & Zatorre, R. J. (2001, 25 Sep). Intensely pleasurable responses to music correlate with activity in brain regions implicated in reward and emotion. *Proceedings of the National Academy of Sciences of the United States of America, 98*(20), 11818–11823.
(Http://www.pnas.org/content/98/20/11818.full.pdf+html)
43. Bloom, P. (2001). Precis of How Children Learn the Meanings of Words. *Behavioral and Brain Sciences, 24,* 1095–1103.
44. Bostock, W. W. (2002, Sep). Atrocity, Mundanity and the Mental Sate. *Journal of Mundane Behavior, 3*(1).
45. Botvinick, M., Nystrom, L. E., Fissell, K., Carter, C. S., & Cohen, J. D. (1999, 11 Nov). Conflict monitoring versus selection-for-action in anterior cingulate cortex. *Nature, 402*(6758), 179–181.
(Http://www.nature.com/nature/journal/v402/n6758/pdf/402179 a0.pdf)
46. Bower, B. (2002, 16 Feb). A Fair Share of the Pie - people everywhere put a social spin on economic exchanges. *Science News.*
47. Bowles, S., & Gintis, H. (2002, 10 Jan). Homo reciprocans. *Nature, 415*(6868), 125–128.
(Http://www.nature.com/nature/journal/v415/n6868/pdf/415125 a.pdf)
48. Bowles, S. (2006, 18 Dec). Group Competition, Reproductive Leveling, and the Evolution of Human Altruism.
Science, 314(5805), 1569–1572.
(Http://www.sciencemag.org/content/314/5805/1569.full.pdf)
49. Bowles, S. (2008, 20 Nov). Conflict: Altruism's midwife. *Nature, 456.*
50. Bowles, S. (2009, 5 Jun). Did Warfare Among Ancestral Hunter-Gatherers Affect the Evolution of Human Social Behaviors? *Science, 324*(5932), 1293–1298.
(Http://www.sciencemag.org/cgi/reprint/324/5932/1293.pdf)
51. Boyd, R., Gintis, H., & Bowles, S. (2010, 30 Apr). Coordinated Punishment of Defectors Sustains Cooperation and Can Proliferate

When Rare. *Science, 328*(5978), 617–620.
(Http://www.sciencemag.org/content/328/5978/617.full.pdf)
52. Brosnan, S. F., & de Waal, F. B. M. (2003, 18 Sep). Monkeys reject unequal pay. *Nature, 425*(6955), 297–299.
(Http://www.nature.com/nature/journal/v425/n6955/pdf/nature0 1963.pdf)
53. Brown, C. M., young, S. G., Sacco, D. F., Bernstein, M. J., & Claypool, H. M. (2009, 1 Jan). Social inclusion facilitates interest in mating. *Evolutionary Psychology, 7*(1), 1–11.
(Http://www.epjournal.net/wp-content/uploads/EP075455592.pdf)
54. Bruce, V., & Young, A. (1998). *In the Eye of the Beholder: The Science of Face Perception.* Oxford: Oxford University Press.
55. Bruna Pelucchi, J. F. H., Jenny R. Saffran. (2009). Statistical Learning in a Natural Language by 8-Month-Old Infants. *Child Development, 80*(3), 674–685.
56. Bryant, J. A., Sanders-Jackson, A., & Smallwood, A. M. (2006). IMing, Text Messaging, and Adolescent Social Networks. *Journal of Computer-Mediated Communication, 11,* 577–592.
57. Buckling, A. (2007, 2 Mar). Keep It Local. *Science, 315,* 1227–8.
(Http://www.sciencemag.org/cgi/reprint/315/5816/1227.pdf)
58. Burke, D., & Sulikowski, D. (2010). A New Viewpoint on the Evolution of Sexually Dimorphic Human Faces. *Evolutionary Psychology, 8*(4), 573–585.
(Http://www.epjournal.net/filestore/EP08573585.pdf?utm_source =MadMimi&utm_medium=email&utm_content=November+2010 +Newsletter&utm_campaign=November+2010+Newsletter&utm_ term=A+new+viewpoint+on+the+evolution+of+sexually+dimorp hic+human+faces_)
59. Burns, L. D. (2013, 9 May). Sustainable mobility: A vision of our transport future. *Nature, 497*(7448), 181–182.
60. Buzsaki, G., & Draguhn, A. (2004, 25 Jun). Neuronal Oscillations in Cortical Networks. *Science, 304*(5679), 1926–1929.
(Http://www.sciencemag.org/cgi/reprint/304/5679/1926.pdf)

61. Caldwell, M. (1995, Jun). Kernel of Fear. *Discover, 16,* 96–102. (Http://discovermagazine.com/1995/jun/kerneloffear519)

62. Cameron, L., Erkal, N., Gangadharan, L., & Meng, X. (2013, 22 Feb). Little Emperors: Behavioral Impacts of China's One-Child Policy. *Science, 339*(6122), 953–957. (Http://www.sciencemag.org/content/339/6122/953.full.pdf)

63. Camilleri, J. A., Kuhlmeier, V. A., & Chu, J. Y. Y. (2010). Remembering helpers and hinderers depends on behavioral intentions of the agent and psychopathic characteristics of the observer. *Evolutionary Psychology, 8*(2), 303–316. (Http://www.epjournal.net/filestore/EP08303316.pdf?utm_source=MadMimi&utm_medium=email&utm_content=July+2010+Newsletter+draft&utm_campaign=July+2010+Newsletter&utm_term=Remembering%2Bhelpers%2Band%2Bhinderers%2Bdepends%2Bon%2Bbehavioral%2Bintentions%2Bof%2Bthe%2Bagent%2Band%2Bpsychopathic%2Bcharacteristics%2Bof%2Bthe%2Bobserver_)

64. Campbell-Meiklejohn, D. K., Bach, D. R., Roepstorff, A., Dolan, R. J., & Frith, C. D. (2010, 13 Aug). How the Opinion of Others Affects Our Valuation of Objects. *Current biology: CB, 20*(13), 1165–1170. (Http://download.cell.com/current-biology/pdf/PIIS0960982210005956.pdf)

65. Canaves, S. (2011, June). What Are You Allowed to Say on China's Social Networks? *ieee Spectrum.* (Http://spectrum.ieee.org/telecom/internet/what-are-you-allowed-to-say-on-chinas-social-networks/0)

66. Carr, N. (2011). *The Shallows: What the Internet Is Doing to Our Brains.* Norton. (Http://www.amazon.com/Shallows-What-Internet-Doing-Brains/dp/0393339750/ref=sr_1_1?ie=UTF8&qid=1421002459&sr=8-1&keywords=nicholas+carr+the+shallows)

67. Carrabis, J., Bratton, S., & Evans, D. (2008, 9 Jun). *Guest Blogger Joseph Carrabis Answers Dave Evans, CEO of Digital Voodoo's Question About Male Executives Weilding Social Media Influence on Par with Female Executives.* The Hungry Peasant. (Http://ttyd.hungrypeasant.com/2016/01/dishymix-guest-blogger-joseph-carrabis-answers-dave-evans-ceo-of-digital-

voodoos-question-about-male-executives-weilding-social-media-influence-on-par-with-female-executives/)

68. Carrabis, J., Carrabis, S., Boone, S., & Ford, W. (2012). *The Heart as a Dollar Sign: Determining the Dollar versus Social Value of Loves, Likes, Followers, Fans, etc., in the Online World.* Critical Mass & NextStage Evolution, LLC.

69. Carrabis, J., & Carrabis, S. (2009). *Designing Information for Automatic Memorization (Branding).* Scotsburn, NS: NextStage Evolution.

70. Carrabis, J., & Carrabis, S. (2009). *Machine Detection of Website Visitor Age and Gender via Analysis of Psychomotor Behavioral Cues.* Scotsburn, NS: Northern Lights Press. (Http://www.nextstagevolution.com/membership.cfm)

71. Carrabis, J., & Peverill-Conti, G. (2011, Oct). The Selling Face - The Selling Face - A Study of Face and Body Biases in Marketing Communications(. *International Journal of Integrated Marketing Communications.*

72. Carrabis, J. (2000). *Thoughts into Movement: The Mechanics of Evolution Technology Part 1 - Modalities and Mathematics.* NextStage Evolution Research Paper.

73. Carrabis, J. (2000). *Thoughts into Movement: The Mechanics of Evolution Technology Part 2 - Browser and Sever Communications.* NextStage Evolution Research Paper.

74. Carrabis, J. (2004, 2006, 2009). *A Primer on Modality Engineering.* NextStage Evolution Research Whitepaper. Scotsburn, NS: Northern Lights Publishing. (Http://www.nextstagevolution.com/membership.cfm)

75. Carrabis, J. (2005, Oct). *Site ReDesign to Facilitate User Migration and Increase Branding.* Hungry Peasant. (Http://bizmediascience.hungrypeasant.com/2014/12/30/site-redesign-to-facilitate-user-migration-and-increase-branding/)

76. Carrabis, J. (2005, 8 Apr). *Usability Studies 101: Brand Loyalty.* IMediaConnections. (Http://www.imediaconnection.com/content/5440.asp)

77. Carrabis, J. (2005, 23 Dec). *Usability Studies 101: Making Cookies from Breadcrumbs.* ImediaConnections. (Http://www.imediaconnection.com/content/7675.asp)

78. Carrabis, J. (2005, 1 July). *Usability Studies 101: The X Funnel*. ImediaConnections. (Http://www.imediaconnection.com/content/6252.asp)

79. Carrabis, J. (2006-). *BizMediaScience Attention Entries*. BizMediaScience. (Http://bizmediascience.hungrypeasant.com/tag/attention/)

80. Carrabis, J. (2006). *Chapter 1, "What this Book is About," Reading Virtual Minds Volume I: Science and History*. Reading Virtual Minds. Nashua, NH: Northern Lights Publishing. (Http://nlb.pub/RVMV14th)

81. Carrabis, J. (2006). *Chapter 2, "History," Reading Virtual Minds Volume I: Science and History*. Scotsburn, NS: Northern Lights Publishing. (Http://nlb.pub/RVMV14th)

82. Carrabis, J. (2006). *Chapter 4 "Anecdotes of Learning," Reading Virtual Minds Volume I: Science and History*. Nashua, NH: Northern Lights Publishing. (Http://nlb.pub/RVMV14th)

83. Carrabis, J. (2006, 2 Dec). *DeBranding, Again...* BizMediaScience. (Http://bizmediascience.hungrypeasant.com/2014/12/30/debranding-again/)

84. Carrabis, J. (2006, 24 Feb). *Focusing Your Customer's Attention*. ImediaConnections. (Http://www.imediaconnection.com/content/8412.asp)

85. Carrabis, J. (2006, May). *Learning to Listen, Learning to See*. Hungry Peasant. (Http://bizmediascience.hungrypeasant.com/2014/12/30/learning-to-listen-learning-to-see/)

86. Carrabis, J. (2006). *A Little About Cookies: A NextStage Evolution Opinion Paper* [NSE Opinion Paper]. NextStage Evolution. Scotsburn, NS: Northern Lights Publishing. (Http://bizmediascience.hungrypeasant.com/2014/12/21/a-little-about-cookies/)

87. Carrabis, J. (2006, 8 Nov). *The Long Tail, Part 1*. BizMediaScience. (Http://www.bizmediascience.com/2006/11/the_long_tail.html)

88. Carrabis, J. (2006, 10 Nov). *Mapping Personae to Outcomes*. (Http://www.imediaconnection.com/content/12358.asp)

89. Carrabis, J. (2006, 8 Dec). *Online Privacy, finale.* BizMediaScience.
(Http://www.bizmediascience.com/2006/12/online_privacy_finale.html)
90. Carrabis, J. (2006). *Reading Virtual Minds Volume I: Science and History, 4th edition.* Nashua, NH: Northern Lights Publishing.
(Http://nlb.pub/RVMV14th)
91. Carrabis, J. (2006, 21 Apr). *Social Networks and Viral Marketing.* IMediaConnection.
(Http://www.imediaconnection.com/content/9195.asp)
92. Carrabis, J. (2006). *Use of Eye Images as Navigation and Action Cues on Websites* [NSE WhitePaper]. NextStage Evolution. Scotsburn, NS: Northern Lights Publishing.
(Http://www.nextstagevolution.com/membership.cfm)
93. Carrabis, J. (2006, 5 May). *Why Some Viral Marketing Doesn't Work.* IMediaConnection.
(Http://www.imediaconnection.com/content/9472.imc)
94. Carrabis, J. (2006, 23 Jun). *Yes, You Can Predict Viral Marketing.* IMediaConnection.
(Http://www.imediaconnection.com//content//10198.asp)
95. Carrabis, J. (2007/2015, 16 May/3 Jan). *The Complete "KBar's Findings: Political Correctness in the Guise of a Sandwich" Arc.* BizMediaScience.
(Http://bizmediascience.hungrypeasant.com/2015/01/03/the-complete-kbars-findings-political-correctness-in-the-guise-of-a-sandwich-arc/)
96. Carrabis, J. (2007/2015, 9 Apr/22 Dec). *The Complete "Notes from UML's Strategic Management Class" Arc.* BizMediaScience.
(Http://bizmediascience.hungrypeasant.com/2015/12/22/the-complete-notes-from-umls-strategic-management-class-arc/)
97. Carrabis, J. (2007/2015, 9 June/21 Dec). *The Complete "Nothing New Under the Sun: Designing for the Small Screen" Arc.* BizMediaScience.
(Http://bizmediascience.hungrypeasant.com/2015/12/21/the-complete-nothing-new-under-the-sun-designing-for-the-small-screen-arc/)

98. Carrabis, J. (2007/2015, 20 June/22 Dec). *The Complete "WindKiller and the Drunken Pirate" Arc.* BizMediaScience. (Http://bizmediascience.hungrypeasant.com/2015/12/22/the-complete-windkiller-and-the-drunken-pirate-arc/)
99. Carrabis, J. (2007/2015, 10 May/3 Jan). *Drunken Pirates, Anyone? or "Interlife Realities 101.".* BizMediaScience. (Http://bizmediascience.hungrypeasant.com/2015/01/03/drunken-pirates-anyone-or-interlife-realities-101/)
100. Carrabis, J. (2007/2015, 30 Mar/22 Dec). *Technology and Buying Patterns.* BizMediaScience. (Http://bizmediascience.hungrypeasant.com/2015/12/22/technology-and-buying-patterns/)
101. Carrabis, J. (2007, 9 Nov). *3 Rules for Engaging Males in Social Site Behavior, Part 1 -- Looking into the Mirror.* AllBusiness.com. (Http://www.allbusiness.com/marketing-advertising/internet-marketing/4968894-1.html)
102. Carrabis, J. (2007, 29 Nov). *Adding sound to your brand website.* ImediaConnections. (Http://www.imediaconnection.com//content//17473.asp)
103. Carrabis, J. (2007, 28 March). *Alarming Results.* (Http://www.bizmediascience.com/2007/03/alarming_results.html)
104. Carrabis, J. (2007). *Attention, Engagement and Trust: The Internet Trinity and Websites.* TriQuatroTriteCale. (Http://triquatrotritecale.hungrypeasant.com/index.php/2013/06/18/attention-engagement-and-trust-the-internet-trinity-and-websites/)
105. Carrabis, J. (2007, 13 Jul). *Attract and Stick, Part 1.* AllBusiness.com. (Http://www.allbusiness.com/marketing-advertising/internet-marketing/4353609-1.html)
106. Carrabis, J. (2007, 27 Jul). *Attract and Stick, Part 2.* AllBusiness.com. (Http://www.allbusiness.com/marketing-advertising/internet-marketing/4353761-1.html)
107. Carrabis, J. (2007-). *BizMediaScience Engagement Archive.* BizMediaScience. (Http://bizmediascience.hungrypeasant.com/tag/engagement/)

108. Carrabis, J. (2007, 14 Jun). *Community Response Grids, Another Example.* BizMediaScience. (Http://bizmediascience.hungrypeasant.com/2015/01/08/community-response-grids-another-example/)

109. Carrabis, J. (2007, Jul). *The Complete "Media Free? That Easy…And Scary. Know Why?" Arc.* BizMediaScience. (Http://bizmediascience.hungrypeasant.com/2014/12/28/the-complete-media-free-that-easy-and-scary-know-why-arc/)

110. Carrabis, J. (2007, 20 April). *Defining Attention on Websites & Blogs.* IMediaConnection. (Http://www.imediaconnection.com//content//14568.asp)

111. Carrabis, J. (2007, 23 Nov). *Engaging Males Through Images.* AllBusiness.com. (Http://www.allbusiness.com/marketing-advertising/internet-marketing/4969186–1.html)

112. Carrabis, J. (2007, 3 Jan). *Implications for Web 2.0 and Rich Media Developers.* Hungry Peasant. (Http://bizmediascience.hungrypeasant.com/2015/01/10/implications-for-web-2–0-and-rich-media-developers/)

113. Carrabis, J. (2007, Oct). *The Importance of Viral Marketing: Podcast and Text.* AllBusiness.com. (Http://www.allbusiness.com/4113507–1.html)

114. Carrabis, J. (2007, 6 Jul). *Intrusive Little Windows or "DeBranding Made Easy.".* AllBusiness.com. (Http://www.allbusiness.com/marketing-advertising/internet-marketing/4353577–1.html)

115. Carrabis, J. (2007, 9 Oct). *Is Social Media a Woman Thing?.* AllBusiness.com. (Http://www.allbusiness.com/marketing-advertising/internet-marketing/4967764–1.html)

116. Carrabis, J. (2007, 11 May). *Make Sure Your Site Sells Lemonade….* IMediaConnections. (Http://www.imediaconnection.com//content//14904.asp)

117. Carrabis, J. (2007, 21 Dec). *Males 3.0.* AllBusiness.com. (Http://www.allbusiness.com/electronics/computer-electronics-manufacturing/5004089–1.html)

118. Carrabis, J. (2007, 5 Dec). *Marketing to men, women and couples.* IMediaConnection.
(Http://www.imediaconnection.com/content/17539.asp)
119. Carrabis, J. (2007, 6 Jun). *Nothing New Under the Sun: Community Response Grids.* BizMediaScience.
(Http://bizmediascience.hungrypeasant.com/2015/01/08/nothing -new-under-the-sun-community-response-grids/)
120. Carrabis, J. (2007, 7 Apr). *Pimp Your Daughter!.* Technology Marketers.
(Http://itknowledgeexchange.techtarget.com/statingtheobvious/p imp-your-daughter/)
121. Carrabis, J. (2007, 27 Aug). *Stonewall's Findings: A New Kind of Community Response Grid.* BizMediaScience.
(Http://bizmediascience.hungrypeasant.com/2015/01/08/stonew alls-findings-a-new-kind-of-community-response-grid/)
122. Carrabis, J. (2007, 24 Aug). *Usability Studies 101: Get the attention you're already paying for.* ImediaConnections.
(Http://www.imediaconnection.com//content//16373.asp)
123. Carrabis, J. (2007, 23 Mar). *Websites: You've Only Got 3 Seconds.* ImediaConnections.
(Http://www.imediaconnection.com/content/7513.asp)
124. Carrabis, J. (2008/2015, 11 Jun/22 Dec). *Rocks, Hammers, Competition and How People Get Left Behind.* BizMediaScience.
(Http://bizmediascience.hungrypeasant.com/2015/12/22/rocks-hammers-competition-and-how-people-get-left-behind/)
125. Carrabis, J. (2008–9, 3 Jul/11 Jul). *From TheFutureOf (10 Jul 08): Back into the fray.* The Analytics Ecology.
(Http://analyticsecology.hungrypeasant.com/index.php/2009/07/ 03/from-thefutureof-10-jul-08-back-into-the-fray/)
126. Carrabis, J. (2008/9, 18 Jul/7 Jul). *From TheFutureOf (16 Jul 08): Responses to Geertz, Papadakis and others, 5 Feb 08.* The Analytics Ecology. (Http://www.theanalyticsecology.com/?p=106)
127. Carrabis, J. (2008/9, 18 Jul/7 Jul). *From TheFutureOf (16 Jul 08): Responses to Papadakis 7 Feb 08.* The Analytics Ecology.
(Http://www.theanalyticsecology.com/?p=104)
128. Carrabis, J. (2008–9, 19 Aug/9 Jul). *From TheFutureOf (19 Aug 08): Response to Visitor Engagement Time for a reality*

check. The Analytics Ecology.
(Http://www.theanalyticsecology.com/?p=123)
129. Carrabis, J. (2008/9, 28 Jan/1 Jul). *From TheFutureOf (22 Jan 08): Starting the discussion: Attention, Engagement, Authority, Influence, ….* The Analytics Ecology.
(Http://www.theanalyticsecology.com/?p=13)
130. Carrabis, J. (2008/9, 29 Aug/9 Jul). *From TheFutureOf (28 Aug 08): Response to Jim Novo's 12 Jul 08 9:40am comment.* The Analytics Ecology.
(Http://www.theanalyticsecology.com/?p=127)
131. Carrabis, J. (2008/9, 10 Nov/15 Jul). *From TheFutureOf (7 Nov 08): Debbie Pascoe asked me to pontificate on "What are we measuring when we measure 'engagement'?".* The Analytics Ecology. (Http://www.theanalyticsecology.com/?p=137)
132. Carrabis, J. (2008, 26 Jun). *The Complete "Canadian Based Business Differences -- Responding to June Li, Christopher Berry and Jaques Warren" Arc (also known as "Responding to Christopher Berry's 'A Vexing Problem.." and incorporating "The Language of Web Analytics - The Hard(er) Sell in Canada").* BizMediaScience.
(Http://bizmediascience.hungrypeasant.com/2015/01/28/the-complete-canadian-based-business-differences-responding-to-june-li-christopher-berry-and-jaques-warren-arc-also-known-as-responding-to-christopher-berrys-a-vexing-problem-and-incorpo/)
133. Carrabis, J. (2008, 1 Oct). *Do McCain, Biden, Palin and Obama Think the Way We Do? (Part 1)The Complete "What is an A6 or A11 or V6 or V21, etc. decision style?" Arc (Originally "Do McCain, Biden, Palin and Obama Think the Way We Do? (Part…)".* BizMediaScience.
(Http://bizmediascience.hungrypeasant.com/2015/01/28/the-complete-what-is-an-a6-or-a11-or-v6-or-v21-etc-decision-style-arc-originally-do-mccain-biden-palin-and-obama-think-the-way-we-do-part/)
134. Carrabis, J. (2008, 31 Oct). *Governor Palin's (and everybody else's) Popularity.* BizMediaScience.

(Http://bizmediascience.hungrypeasant.com/2015/03/14/governo
r-palins-and-everybody-elses-popularity/)
135. Carrabis, J. (2008, 24 Oct). *How OJ Simpson Won Barack
Obama the 2008 Presidential Election.* BizMediaScience.
(Http://www.bizmediascience.com/2008/10/how_oj_simpson_wo
n_barack_obam.html)
136. Carrabis, J. (2008, 31 July). *Programable method and
apparatus for real-time adaptation of presentations to individuals
(Patent #1).* US Patent Office (USPTO.GOV).
(Http://appft.uspto.gov/netacgi/nph-
Parser?Sect1=PTO2&Sect2=HITOFF&p=1&u=%2Fnetahtml%2FPT
O%2Fsearch-
bool.html&r=2&f=G&l=50&co1=AND&d=PG01&s1=Carrabis&OS=
Carrabis&RS=Carrabis)
137. Carrabis, J. (2008, 21 Jan). *VerizonWireless' 20 year plan.*
AllBusiness.com. (Http://www.allbusiness.com/media-
telecommunications/telecommunications/6347110–1.html)
138. Carrabis, J. (2009/2015, 10 Nov/22 Dec). *Counting
Wristwatches at the SNCR Conference.* BizMediaScience.
(Http://bizmediascience.hungrypeasant.com/2015/12/22/countin
g-wristwatches-at-the-sncr-conference/)
139. Carrabis, J. (2009/2015, 5 Jun/8 Jan). *Sentiment Analysis,
Anyone? (Part 1).* BizMediaScience.
(Http://bizmediascience.hungrypeasant.com/2015/01/08/sentime
nt-analysis-anyone-part-1/)
140. Carrabis, J. (2009, 12 Jun). *Canoeing with Stephane
(Sentiment Analysis, Anyone? (Part 2)).* BizMediaScience.
(Http://bizmediascience.hungrypeasant.com/2015/01/29/canoein
g-with-stephane-sentiment-analysis-anyone-part-2/)
141. Carrabis, J. (2009). *A Demonstration of Professional Test-
Taker Bias in Web-Based Panels and Applications.* San Francisco,
CA: Society for New Communications Research.
142. Carrabis, J. (2009). *Frequency of Blog Posts is Best
Determined by Audience Size and Psychological Distance from the
Author.* Scotsburn, NS: NextStage Evolution.
(Http://www.nextstagevolution.com/membership.cfm)

143. Carrabis, J. (2009, 1 Oct). *Learning to Use New Tools.* The Analytics Ecology. (Http://www.theanalyticsecology.com/?p=152)
144. Carrabis, J. (2009). Machine Detection of and Response to User Non-Conscious Thought Processes to Increase Usability, Experience and Satisfaction - Case Studies and Examples. In *The 2nd International Multi-Conference on Engineering and Technological Innovation* (Vol. 3, pp. 69–74). Orlando, FL: International Institute of Informatics and Systemics.
145. Carrabis, J. (2010, 2 Feb). *Five Rules Re: Online Visibility Versus Privacy.* AllBusiness.com.
(Http://www.allbusiness.com/population-demographics/population-size/13412393–1.html)
146. Carrabis, J. (2010, 20 Jul). *"It's too accurate" (more undocumented uses of NextStage's Evolution Technology).* Hungry Peasant (Triquatrotritecale).
(Http://triquatrotritecale.hungrypeasant.com/?p=110)
147. Carrabis, J. (2010, 26 Oct). *Programmable method and apparatus for real-time adaptation of presentations to individuals (Patent #2).* US Patent Office (USPTO.GOV).
(Http://patft.uspto.gov/netacgi/nph-Parser?Sect1=PTO2&Sect2=HITOFF&p=1&u=%2Fnetahtml%2FPTO%2Fsearch-bool.html&r=1&f=G&l=50&co1=AND&d=PTXT&s1=carrabis&OS=carrabis&RS=carrabis)
148. Carrabis, J. (2010). *Social Network Mechanics: A Preliminary ToolKit for Creating and Co-Opting Social Networks for Marketing Purposes.* Scotsburn, NS: NextStage Evolution.
(Http://www.nextstagevolution.com/membership.cfm)
149. Carrabis, J. (2010, 18 Feb). *The Unfulfilled Promise of Online Analytics, Part 3 – Determining the Human Cost.* The Analytics Ecology.
(Http://www.theanalyticsecology.com/index.php/2010/02/18/the-unfulfilled-promise-of-online-analytics-part-3-determining-the-human-cost/)
150. Carrabis, J. (2011, 7 Mar). *Elementary Linguistics in the Information Age (WE'RE LOSING!).* AllBusiness.com.

(Http://www.allbusiness.com/humanities-social-
science/linguistics/15479522–1.html)
151. Carrabis, J. (2011, 1 Jul). *When it's OK to confuse your
customers.* IMediaConnection.
(Http://www.imediaconnection.com/content/29459.asp)
152. Carrabis, J. (2012, 18 Dec). *System and Method for
Obtaining Subtextual Information Regarding an Interaction
Between an Individual and a Programmable Device (Patent #3).*
US Patent Office (USPTO.GOV).
(Http://appft.uspto.gov/netacgi/nph-
Parser?Sect1=PTO2&Sect2=HITOFF&p=1&u=%2Fnetahtml%2FPT
O%2Fsearch-
bool.html&r=1&f=G&l=50&co1=AND&d=PG01&s1=Carrabis&OS=
Carrabis&RS=Carrabis)
153. Carrabis, J. (2013, 9 Oct). *Digital Divisivity.* An Economy of
Meanings.
(Http://aneconomyofmeaning.wordpress.com/2013/10/09/digital-
divisivity/)
154. Carrabis, J. (2013, 23 Oct). *Joseph Carrabis' Under the
Influence: Customer Service, Acquisition and Retention in the Age
of Digital Divisivity.* IMediaConnection.
(Http://blogs.imediaconnection.com/blog/2013/10/23/joseph-
carrabis-under-the-influence-customer-service-acquisition-and-
retention-in-the-age-of-digital-divisivity/)
155. Carrabis, J. (2014, 5 Feb). *12 Mobile Marketing Secrets You
Need to Know.* IMediaConnection.
(Http://www.imediaconnection.com/content/35876.asp#multivie
w)
156. Carrabis, J. (2014, 4 Jun). *This puts a whole new meaning
on impatience, doesn't it?.* LinkedIn.
(Https://www.linkedin.com/today/post/article/20140604195942–
112718-this-puts-a-whole-new-meaning-on-impatience-doesn-t-
it?trk=mp-author-card)
157. Carrabis, J. (2015). *Reading Virtual Minds Volume II:
Experience and Expectation.* Nashua. NH: Northern Lights
Publishing. (Http://www.amazon.com/Reading-Virtual-Minds-
Joseph-Carrabis/dp/0984140301)

158. Carrabis, S. (2007). *DeBranding.* Hungry Peasant. (Http://bizmediascience.hungrypeasant.com/2015/01/05/debranding/)

159. Carter, R. M., Bowling, D. L., Reeck, C., & Huettel, S. A. (2012, 6 Jul). A Distinct Role of the Temporal-Parietal Junction in Predicting Socially Guided Decisions. *Science, 337*(6090), 109–111. (Http://www.sciencemag.org/content/337/6090/109.full.pdf)

160. Centola, D. (2010, 3 Sep). The Spread of Behavior in an Online Social Network Experiment. *Science, 329*(5996), 1194–1197. (Http://www.sciencemag.org/content/329/5996/1194.full.pdf)

161. Cerf, M., Thiruvengadam, N., Mormann, F., Kraskov, A., Quiroga, R. Q., Koch, C., et al. (2010, 28 Oct). On-line, voluntary control of human temporal lobe neurons. *Nature, 467*(7319), 1104–1108. (Http://www.nature.com/nature/journal/v467/n7319/pdf/nature09510.pdf)

162. Cha, J. (2010, 6 Dec). Factors affecting the frequency and amount of social networking site use: Motivations, perceptions, and privacy concerns. *First Monday, 15*(12). (Http://firstmonday.org/htbin/cgiwrap/bin/ojs/index.php/fm/article/view/2889/2685)

163. Chan, L., & Costa, S. (2005). Participation in the global knowledge commons: Challenges and opportunities for research dissemination in developing countries. *New Library World, 106*(s 3–4), 141–163.

164. Charron, S., & Koechlin, E. (2010, 16 Apr). Divided Representation of Concurrent Goals in the Human Frontal Lobes. *Science, 328*(5976), 360–363. (Http://www.sciencemag.org/content/328/5976/360.full.pdf)

165. Chen, L. M., Friedman, R. M., & Roe, A. W. (2003, 31 Oct). Optical Imaging of a Tactile Illusion in Area 3b of the Primary Somatosensory Cortex. *Science, 302*(5646), 881–885. (Http://www.sciencemag.org/cgi/reprint/sci;302/5646/881.pdf)

166. Chli, M., & De Wilde, P. (2006). *The emergence of knowledge exchange: An agent-based model of a software market.*

167. Cho, A. (2011, 13 May). Scientific Link-Up Yields 'Control Panel' for Networks. *Science, 332*(6031), 777–777. (Http://www.sciencemag.org/content/332/6031/777.full.pdf)

168. Choi, J.-K., & Bowles, S. (2007, 26 Oct). The Coevolution of Parochial Altruism and War. *Science, 318*(5850), 636–640. (Http://www.sciencemag.org/content/318/5850/636.full.pdf)

169. Chris Fullwood, Mike Thelwall, & Sam O'Neill. (2011, 2 May). Clandestine chatters: Self-disclosure in U.K. chat room profiles. *First Monday, 16*(5). (Http://firstmonday.org/htbin/cgiwrap/bin/ojs/index.php/fm/article/view/3231/2954)

170. Ciotti, G. (2013, 6 Mar). *Why Steve Jobs Didn't Listen to His Customers.* Help Scout. (Http://www.helpscout.net/blog/why-steve-jobs-never-listened-to-his-customers/)

171. Clark, L., Ting, I.-H., Kimble, C., Wright, P., & Kudenko, D. (2006, Jan). Combining ethnographic and clickstream data to identify user Web browsing strategies. *informationresearch, 11*(2).

172. Clutton-Brock, T. (2002, 5 Apr). Breeding Together: Kin Selection and Mutualism in Cooperative Vertebrates. *Science, 296*(5565), 69–72. (10.1126/science.296.5565.69)

173. Clutton-Brock, T. (2009, 5 Nov). Cooperation between non-kin in animal societies. *Nature, 462*(7269), 51–57. (Http://www.nature.com/nature/journal/v462/n7269/pdf/nature08366.pdf)

174. Cohn, A., Fehr, E., & Marechal, M. A. (2014, 4 Dec). Business culture and dishonesty in the banking industry. *Nature, 516*(7529), 86–89. (Http://www.nature.com/nature/journal/v516/n7529/pdf/nature13977.pdf)

175. Connor, T. (2006). *Tom Connor's Thinking Forward: The Value of Money.* Hungry Peasant. (Http://www.hungrypeasant.com/pdfdownload.cfm?thisone=articles/TomConnor/TomConnorThinkingForwardValueofMoney.pdf)

176. Connor, T. (2006). *Tom Connor's Thinking Foward: Trust Matters.* Hungry Peasant.
(Http://www.hungrypeasant.com/pdfdownload.cfm?thisone=articl es/TomConnor/TomConnorThinkingForwardTrustMatters.pdf)
177. Conway, C., Jones, B., DeBruine, L., & Little, A. (2008, 7 Jul). Evidence for adaptive design in human gaze preference. *Proceedings of the Royal Society B: Biological Sciences, 275*(1630), 63–69.
(Http://rspb.royalsocietypublishing.org/content/275/1630/63.full. pdf+html)
178. Conway, C. M., & Christiansen, M. H. (2006, 1 Oct). Statistical Learning Within and Between Modalities: Pitting Abstract Against Stimulus-Specific Representations. *Psychological Science, 17*(10), 905–912.
179. Cooperation evolves via reward strategy. (1993, 3 Jul). *Science News,* p. 1.
(Http://www.thefreelibrary.com/Cooperation+evolves+via+rewar d+strategy-a014067470)
180. Corabi, J. (2008). Pleasure's Role In Evolution: A Response To Robinson. *Journal of Consciousness Studies, 15*(7), 78–86.
(Http://www.ingentaconnect.com/content/imp/jcs/2008/0000001 5/00000007/art00003)
181. Cornwallis, C. K., West, S. A., Davis, K. E., & Griffin, A. S. (2010, 19 Aug). Promiscuity and the evolutionary transition to complex societies. *Nature, 466*(7309), 969–972.
(Http://www.nature.com/nature/journal/v466/n7309/pdf/nature0 9335.pdf)
182. Coull, J. T., Vidal, F., Nazarian, B., & Macar, F. (2004, 5 Mar). Functional Anatomy of the Attentional Modulation of Time Estimation. *Science, 303*(5663), 1506–1508.
(Http://www.sciencemag.org/cgi/reprint/sci;303/5663/1506.pdf)
183. Coward, F. (2008, 14 Mar). Standing on the Shoulders of Giants. *Science, 319*(5869), 1493–1495.
(Http://www.sciencemag.org/content/319/5869/1493.full.pdf)
184. Cox, D., Meyers, E., & Sinha, P. (2004, 2 Apr). Contextually Evoked Object-Specific Responses in Human Visual Cortex.

Science, 304(5667), 115–117.
(Http://www.sciencemag.org/cgi/reprint/sci;304/5667/115.pdf)
185. Crisp, R. J., & Meleady, R. (2012, 18 May). Adapting to a
Multicultural Future. *Science, 336*(6083), 853–855.
(Http://www.sciencemag.org/content/336/6083/853.full.pdf)
186. Crocker, L. D., Heller, W., Warren, S. L., O'Hare, A. J.,
Infantolino, Z. P., & Miller, G. A. (2013, 11 Jun). Relationships
among cognition, emotion, and motivation: Implications for
intervention and neuroplasticity in psychopathology. *Frontiers in
Human Neuroscience, 7.*
(Http://www.frontiersin.org/Journal/DownloadFile.ashx?pdf=1&Fil
eId=256953&articleId=47185&Version=1&ContentTypeId=21&Fil
eName=fnhum-07-00261.pdf)
187. Cross, I. (2001, June). Music, Cognition, Culture, and
Evolution. *Annals of the New York Academy of
Sciences, 930*(1), 28–42.
(Http://onlinelibrary.wiley.com/doi/10.1111/j.1749–
6632.2001.tb05723.x/pdf)
188. David Cesarini, Christopher T. Dawes, Magnus Johannesson,
Paul Lichtenstein, & Björn Wallace. (2009). Experimental Game
Theory and Behavior Genetics. *Annals of the New York Academy
of Sciences, 1167*(Values, Empathy, and Fairness across Social
Barriers), 66–75. (Http://www3.interscience.wiley.com/cgi-
bin/fulltext/122466386/PDFSTART)
189. Daw, N. D., & Dayan, P. (2004, 18 Jun). Matchmaking.
Science, 304(5678), 1753–1754.
(Http://www.sciencemag.org/cgi/reprint/304/5678/1753.pdf)
190. de Irala, J., Osorio, A., Carlos, S., Ruiz-Canela, M., & López-
del Burgo, C. (2011–10–01). Mean Age of First Sex: Do They
Know What We Mean? *Archives of Sexual Behavior, 40*(5), 853–
855. Springer Netherlands.
191. de Quervain, D. J.-F., Fischbacher, U., Treyer, V.,
Schellhammer, M., Schnyder, U., Buck, A., et al. (2004, 27 Aug).
The Neural Basis of Altruistic Punishment.
Science, 305(5688), 1254–1258.
(Http://www.sciencemag.org/cgi/reprint/sci;305/5688/1254.pdf)

192. De Smedt, J., & De Cruz, H. (2010, Dec). Toward an integrative approach of cognitive neuroscientific and evolutionary psychological studies of art. *Evolutionary Psychology, 8*(4), 695–719.
(Http://www.epjournal.net/filestore/EP08695719.pdf?utm_source =MadMimi&utm_medium=email&utm_content=December+2010 +Newsletter&utm_campaign=December+2010+Newsletter&utm_ term=Toward+an+integrative+approach+of+cognitive+neuroscie ntific+and+evolutionary+psychological+studies+of+art_)
193. de Waal, F. B. M., & Berger, M. L. (2000, 6 Apr). Payment for labour in monkeys. *Nature, 404*(6778), 563–563.
(Http://www.nature.com/nature/journal/v404/n6778/pdf/404563 a0.pdf)
194. Dean, L. G., Kendal, R. L., Schapiro, S. J., Thierry, B., & Laland, K. N. (2012, 2 Mar). Identification of the Social and Cognitive Processes Underlying Human Cumulative Culture. *Science, 335*(6072), 1114–1118.
(Http://www.sciencemag.org/content/335/6072/1114.full.pdf)
195. DeBruine, L. M., Jones, B. C., Crawford, J. R., Welling, L. L. M., & Little, A. C. (2010, 7 Aug). The health of a nation predicts their mate preferences: Cross-cultural variation in women's preferences for masculinized male faces. *Proceedings of the Royal Society B: Biological Sciences, 277*(1692), 2405–2410.
(Http://rspb.royalsocietypublishing.org/content/277/1692/2405.f ull.pdf+html)
196. DeBruine, L. M., Jones, B. C., Little, A. C., Boothroyd, L. G., Perrett, D. I., Penton-Voak, I. S., et al. (2006, 7 Jun). Correlated preferences for facial masculinity and ideal or actual partner's masculinity. *Proceedings of the Royal Society B: Biological Sciences, 273*(1592), 1355–1360.
(Http://rspb.royalsocietypublishing.org/content/273/1592/1355.f ull.pdf+html)
197. DeBruine, L. M., Jones, B. C., Little, A. C., Crawford, J. R., & Welling, L. L. M. (2011, 22 Mar). Further evidence for regional variation in women's masculinity preferences. *Proceedings of the Royal Society B: Biological Sciences, 278*(1707), 813–814.

(Http://rspb.royalsocietypublishing.org/content/278/1707/813.ful
l.pdf+html)
198. DeBruine, L. M. (2002, 7 Jul). Facial resemblance enhances
trust. *Proceedings of the Royal Society of London. Series B:
Biological Sciences, 269*(1498), 1307–1312.
(Http://rspb.royalsocietypublishing.org/content/269/1498/1307.f
ull.pdf+html)
199. DeBruine, L. M. (2004, 7 Oct). Facial resemblance increases
the attractiveness of same-sex faces more than other-sex faces.
*Proceedings of the Royal Society of London. Series B: Biological
Sciences, 271*(1552), 2085–2090.
(Http://rspb.royalsocietypublishing.org/content/271/1552/2085.f
ull.pdf+html)
200. Decety, J., Grezes, J., Costes, N., Perani, D., Jeannerod, M.,
Procyk, E., et al. (1997). Brain activity during observation of
actions (Influence of action content and subject's strategy).
Brain, 120, 1763–1777.
201. Dede, C. Immersive Interfaces for Engagement and
Learning. *Science, 323*(5910), 66–69.
(Http://www.sciencemag.org/cgi/reprint/323/5910/66.pdf)
202. Dedre Gentner, L. L. N. (2006). Analogical Processes in
Language Learning. *Current Directions in Psychological
Science, 15*(6), 297–301.
(Http://www3.interscience.wiley.com/cgi-
bin/fulltext/118584118/PDFSTART)
203. Dehaene, S., Pegado, F., Braga, L. W., Ventura, P., Filho, G.
N., Jobert, A., et al. (2010, 3 Dec). How Learning to Read
Changes the Cortical Networks for Vision and Language.
Science, 330(6009), 1359–1364.
(Http://www.sciencemag.org/content/330/6009/1359.full.pdf)
204. Delfanti, A. (2013). *Biohackers: The Politics of Open
Science.* Pluto Press. (Http://www.amazon.com/Biohackers-
Politics-Science-Alessandro-
Delfanti/dp/0745332803/ref=sr_1_1?s=books&ie=UTF8&qid=142
0409867&sr=1–
1&keywords=Biohackers+The+Politics+of+Open+Science)

205. DellaVigna, S. (2010, 16 Jul). Consumers Who Care. *Science, 329*(5989), 287–288. (Http://www.sciencemag.org/content/329/5989/287.full.pdf)
206. Delton, A. W., & Cimino, A. (2010). Exploring the evolved concept of NEWCOMER: Experimental tests of a cognitive model. *Evolutionary Psychology, 8*(2), 317–335. (Http://www.epjournal.net/filestore/EP08317335.pdf?utm_source =MadMimi&utm_medium=email&utm_content=July+2010+Newsl etter+draft&utm_campaign=July+2010+Newsletter&utm_term=E xploring%2Bthe%2Bevolved%2Bconcept%2Bof%2BNEWCOMER% 253A%2BExperimental%2Btests%2Bof%2Ba%2Bcognitive%2Bm odel_)
207. Denning, S. (2014). An economy of access is opening for business: Five strategies for success. *Strategy and Leadership, 42*(4), 14–21. (Http://www.ingentaconnect.com/search/article?option1=tka&val ue1=%22sharing+economy%22&pageSize=10&index=4)
208. Deodato, J. (2014). The patron as producer: Libraries, web 2.0, and participatory culture. *Journal of Documentation, 70*(5), 734–758.
209. Derex, M., Beugin, M.-P., Godelle, B., & Raymond, M. (2013, 21 Nov). Experimental evidence for the influence of group size on cultural complexity. *Nature, 503*(7476), 389–391. (Http://www.nature.com/nature/journal/v503/n7476/pdf/nature1 2774.pdf)
210. Deron, M. (2000, Jan). How Important is Visual Feedback When Using a TouchScreen? *Usability News, 2*(1).
211. Diedrichsen, J., Hashambhoy, Y., Rane, T., & Shadmehr, R. (2005, 26 Oct). Neural Correlates of Reach Errors. *The Journal of Neuroscience, 25*(43), 9919–9931. (Http://www.jneurosci.org/content/25/43/9919.full.pdf+html)
212. Dixson, B., Grimshaw, G., Linklater, W., & Dixson, A. (2011, 1 Feb). Eye Tracking of Men's Preferences for Female Breast Size and Areola Pigmentation. *Archives of Sexual Behavior, 40*(1), 51–58. Springer Netherlands.
213. Dixson, B., Grimshaw, G., Linklater, W., & Dixson, A. (2011, 1 Feb). Eye-Tracking of Men's Preferences for Waist-to-Hip Ratio

and Breast Size of Women. *Archives of Sexual Behavior, 40*(1), 43–50. Springer Netherlands.

214. Dodds, P. S., Muhamad, R., & Watts, D. J. (2003, 8 Aug). An Experimental Study of Search in Global Social Networks. *Science, 301*(5634), 827–829. (Http://www.sciencemag.org/cgi/reprint/sci;301/5634/827.pdf)

215. Doebeli, M., Hauert, C., & Killingback, T. (2004, 29 Oct). The Evolutionary Origin of Cooperators and Defectors. *Science, 306*(5697), 859–862. (Http://www.sciencemag.org/content/306/5697/859.full.pdf)

216. Doidge, N. (2007). *The Brain That Changes Itself.* Penguin Books. (Http://www.amazon.com/Brain-That-Changes-Itself-Frontiers/dp/0143113100/ref=sr_1_1?s=books&ie=UTF8&qid=13 74783048&sr=1-1&keywords=the+brain+that+changes+itself)

217. Dolen, G., Darvishzadeh, A., Huang, K. W., & Malenka, R. C. (2013, 13 Sep). Social reward requires coordinated activity of nucleus accumbens oxytocin and serotonin. *Nature, 501*(7466), 179–184.

218. Downing, P. E., Jiang, Y., Shuman, M., & Kanwisher, N. (2001, 28 Sep). A Cortical Area Selective for Visual Processing of the Human Body. *Science, 293*(5539), 2470–2473. (Http://www.sciencemag.org/cgi/reprint/sci;293/5539/2470.pdf)

219. Draaisma, D. (2001, 8 Nov). The tracks of thought. *Nature, 414*(6860), 153–153. (Http://www.nature.com/nature/journal/v414/n6860/pdf/414153 a0.pdf)

220. Dranovsky, A., Picchini, A., Moadel, T., Sisti, A., Yamada, A., Kimura, S., et al. (2011, 9 Jun). Experience Dictates Stem Cell Fate in the Adult Hippocampus. *Neuron, 70*(5), 908–923. (Http://linkinghub.elsevier.com/retrieve/pii/S0896627311004405)

221. Durand, E., Blum, M., & Francois, O. (2006). *A mean-field analysis of community structure in social and kin networks.* Cornell University Library. (Http://arxiv.org/pdf/q-bio/0604016v1)

222. Dye, C. D., Walenski, M., Prado, E. L., Mostofsky, S., & Ullman, M. T. (2013, 9 Sep). Children's Computation of Complex

Linguistic Forms: A Study of Frequency and Imageability Effects. *PLoS ONE, 8*(9).
223. Edvardsson, B., & Gustafsson, A. (2007). Analysis Of Triggers For Customer Switching Path - A Case Study At Volvo Car Corporation. Karlstad University: Karlstad University.
224. Efferson, C., Lalive, R., & Fehr, E. (2008, 26 Sep). The Coevolution of Cultural Groups and Ingroup Favoritism. *Science, 321*(5897), 1844–1849. (Http://www.sciencemag.org/content/321/5897/1844.full.pdf)
225. Emlen, S. T. (1995, 29 Aug). An evolutionary theory of the family. *Proceedings of the National Academy of Sciences of the United States of America, 92*(18), 8092–8099. (Http://www.pnas.org/content/92/18/8092.full.pdf+html)
226. Ernst, M. O., & Banks, M. S. (2002, 24 Jan). Humans integrate visual and haptic information in a statistically optimal fashion. *Nature, 415,* 429–433.
227. Estévez, M., & Fabrizio, D. (2014, Jul). Advertising Effectiveness: An Approach Based on What Consumers Perceive and What Advertisers Need. *Open Journal of Business and Management, 2*(3), 180–188. (Http://www.scirp.org/journal/PaperDownload.aspx?paperID=475 88)
228. Esther M. Leerkes, A. N. B., Marion O'Brien. (2009). Differential Effects of Maternal Sensitivity to Infant Distress and Nondistress on Social-Emotional Functioning. *Child Development, 80*(3), 762–775.
229. Etcoff, N. (1999). *Survival of the Prettiest: The Science of Beauty.* NYC: Doubleday.
230. Ethofer, T., Van De Ville, D., Scherer, K., & Vuilleumier, P. (2009, 23 Jun). Decoding of Emotional Information in Voice-Sensitive Cortices. *Current Biology, 19*(12), 1028–1033. (Http://www.sciencedirect.com/science?_ob=ArticleURL&_udi=B6 VRT-4W929HC-4&_user=10&_coverDate=06%2F23%2F2009&_rdoc=1&_fmt=hi gh&_orig=browse&_sort=d&view=c&_acct=C000050221&_versio n=1&_urlVersion=0&_userid=10&md5=a57e07a3255950cfe2327 d7f453d588e)

231. Evans, J. (2007). *Modelling the Relationship Between Psychic Distance and Organisational Performance.* Manchester Metropolitan University Business School.

232. Eyal, T., Sagristano, M. D., Trope, Y., Liberman, N., & Chaiken, S. (2008, 14 Mar). When Values Matter: Expressing Values in Behavioral Intentions for the Near vs. Distant Future. *Journal of Experimental Social Psychology, 45,* 35–43.

233. Falk, H. (2005). State library databases on the internet. *The Electronic Library, 23*(4), 492–498.

234. Fara, P. (2003, 7 Feb). Face Values: How Portraits Win Friends and Influence People. *Science, 299*(5608), 831–832. (Http://www.sciencemag.org/cgi/reprint/sci;299/5608/831.pdf)

235. Fehr, E., & Fischbacher, U. (2003, 23 Oct). The nature of human altruism. *Nature, 425*(6960), 785–791. (Http://www.nature.com/nature/journal/v425/n6960/pdf/nature0 2043.pdf)

236. Fehr, E., & Gachter, S. (2002, 10 Jan). Altruistic punishment in humans. *Nature, 415*(6868), 137–140. (Http://www.nature.com/nature/journal/v415/n6868/pdf/415137 a.pdf)

237. Fehr, E., & Rockenbach, B. (2003, 13 Mar). Detrimental effects of sanctions on human altruism. *Nature, 422*(6928), 137–140. (Http://www.nature.com/nature/journal/v422/n6928/pdf/nature0 1474.pdf)

238. Fehr, E. (2004, 15 Apr). The productivity of failures. *Nature, 428*(6984), 701–701. (Http://www.nature.com/nature/journal/v428/n6984/pdf/428701 a.pdf)

239. Feng, J., Spence, I., & Pratt, J. (2007, 1 Oct). Playing an Action Video Game Reduces Gender Differences in Spatial Cognition. *Psychological Science, 18*(10), 850–855. (Http://pss.sagepub.com/content/18/10/850.full.pdf+html)

240. Fenske, M. J., Raymond, J. E., Kessler, K., Westoby, N., & Tipper, S. E. (2005, Oct). Attentional Inhibition Has Social-Emotional Consequences for Unfamiliar Faces. *Psychological Science, 16*(10), 753–758.

(Http://www3.interscience.wiley.com/cgi-bin/fulltext/118661655/PDFSTART)

241. Fernandez-Duque, D., & Posner, M. (1997, 28 Feb). Relating the mechanisms of orienting and alerting. *Neuropsychologia, 35*(4), 477–486.

242. Ferster, D. (2004, 12 Mar). Blocking Plasticity in the Visual Cortex. *Science, 303*(5664), 1619–1621. (Http://www.sciencemag.org/cgi/reprint/303/5664/1619.pdf)

243. Fiegna, F., Yu, Y.-T. N., Kadam, S. V., & Velicer, G. J. (2006, 18 May). Evolution of an obligate social cheater to a superior cooperator. *Nature, 441*(7091), 310–314. (Http://www.nature.com/nature/journal/v441/n7091/pdf/nature04677.pdf)

244. Field, J., Cronin, A., & Bridge, C. (2006, 11 May). Future fitness and helping in social queues. *Nature, 441*(7090), 214–217. (Http://www.nature.com/nature/journal/v441/n7090/pdf/nature04560.pdf)

245. Finn Brunton, & Helen Nissenbaum. (2011, 2 May). Vernacular resistance to data collection and analysis: A political theory of obfuscation. *First Monday, 16*(5). (Http://firstmonday.org/htbin/cgiwrap/bin/ojs/index.php/fm/article/view/3493/2955)

246. Fitzgerald, C., J., Thompson, M., C., & Whitaker, M., B. (2010, Sep). Altruism between Romantic Partners: Biological Offspring as a Genetic Bridge between Altruist and Recipient. *Evolutionary Psychology, 8*(3), 462–476. (Http://www.epjournal.net/filestore/EP08462476.pdf?utm_source=MadMimi&utm_medium=email&utm_content=September+2010+Newsletter&utm_campaign=September+2010+Newsletter&utm_term=Altruism%2Bbetween%2Bromantic%2Bpartners_3A%2BBiological%2Boffspring%2Bas%2Ba%2Bgenetic%2Bbridge%2Bbetween%2Baltruist%2Band%2Brecipient_)

247. Fitzgerald, C. J., & Whitaker, M. B. (2009). Sex Differences in Violent versus Non-Violent Life-Threatening Altruism. *Evolutionary Psychology, 7*(3), 467–476. (Http://www.epjournal.net/filestore/ep07467476.pdf)

248. Fossett, M. (1999). Ethnic Preferences, Social Distance Dynamics, and Residential Segregation: Results from Simulation Analyses. Annual Meetings of the American Sociological Association, Chicago, IL: Texas A&M University.

249. Fraccaro, P. J., Feinberg, D. R., DeBruine, L. M., Little, A. C., Watkins, C. D., & Jones, B. C. (2010, Sep). Correlated Male Preferences for Femininity in Female Faces and Voices. *Evolutionary Psychology, 8*(3), 447–461. (Http://www.epjournal.net/filestore/EP08447461.pdf?utm_source =MadMimi&utm_medium=email&utm_content=September+2010 +Newsletter&utm_campaign=September+2010+Newsletter&utm _term=Correlated%2Bmale%2Bpreferences%2Bfor%2Bfemininity %2Bin%2Bfemale%2Bfaces%2Band%2Bvoices_)

250. Frankel, M. S., & Siang, S. (1999). *Ethical and Legal Aspects of Human Subjects Research on the Internet.* Washington, DC: Scientific Freedom, Responsibility and Law Program/Directorate of Science and Policy Programs/American Association for the Advancement of Science.

251. Friesen, N. (2010, 6 Dec). Education and the social Web: Connective learning and the commercial imperative. *First Monday, 15*(12). (Http://firstmonday.org/htbin/cgiwrap/bin/ojs/index.php/fm/artic le/view/3149/2718)

252. Furlong, E. E., & Opfer, J. E. (2009). Cognitive Constraints on How Economic Rewards Affect Cooperation. *Psychological Science,* p. 8.

253. Gachter, S., Renner, E., & Sefton, M. (2008, 5 Dec). The Long-Run Benefits of Punishment. *Science, 322.* (Http://www.sciencemag.org/content/322/5907/1510.full.pdf?sid =13367aca-3636–4065–8593–3d4ca9807c15)

254. Gaffan, D. (2005, 30 Sep). Widespread Cortical Networks Underlie Memory and Attention. *Science, 309*(5744), 2172–2173. (Http://www.sciencemag.org/cgi/reprint/309/5744/2172.pdf)

255. Gallup, A. C., O'Brien, D. T., White, D. D., & Wilson, D. S. (2010, Jun). Handgrip strength and socially dominant behavior in male adolescents. *Evolutionary Psychology, 8*(2), 229–244. (Http://www.epjournal.net/filestore/EP08229244.pdf?utm_source

=MadMimi&utm_medium=email&utm_content=June+2010+News letter&utm_campaign=June+2010+Newsletter&utm_term=Handg rip%2Bstrength%2Band%2Bsocially%2Bdominant%2Bbehavior% 2Bin%2Bmale%2Badolescents_)
256. Gardner, A., & West, S. A. (2004, 3 Sep). Spite Among Siblings. *Science, 305*(5689), 1413–1414. (Http://www.sciencemag.org/cgi/reprint/sci;305/5689/1413.pdf)
257. Gelman, A. (2007). Methodology as ideology: Mathematical modeling of trench warfare. NYC: Columbia.
258. Gilbert, C. D., Sigman, M., & Crist, R. E. (2001, 13 Sep). The Neural Basis of Perceptual Learning. *Neuron, 31*(5), 681–697. (Http://linkinghub.elsevier.com/retrieve/pii/S089662730100424X)
259. Gilbert, D. T., Killingsworth, M. A., Eyre, R. N., & Wilson, T. D. (2009, 20 Mar). The Surprising Power of Neighborly Advice. *Science, 323*(5921), 1617–1619. (Http://www.sciencemag.org/cgi/reprint/sci;323/5921/1617.pdf)
260. Glanville R. (2002). A (Cybernetic) Musing: Cybernetics and Human Knowing. *Cybernetics & Human Knowing, 9*(1), 75–82. (Http://www.ingentaconnect.com/content/imp/chk/2002/000000 09/00000001/109)
261. Gneezy, A., Gneezy, U., Nelson, L. D., & Brown, A. (2010, 16 Jul). Shared Social Responsibility: A Field Experiment in Pay-What-You-Want Pricing and Charitable Giving. *Science, 329*(5989), 325–327. (Http://www.sciencemag.org/content/329/5989/325.full.pdf)
262. Gneezy, U., Keenan, E. A., & Gneezy, A. (2014, 31 Oct). Avoiding overhead aversion in charity. *Science, 346*(6209), 632–635. (Http://www.sciencemag.org/content/346/6209/632.full.pdf)
263. Goldman, J. G. (2010, 20 Sep). *Proto-Fairness? Hints of Moral Thinking in Dogs.* Http://scienceblogs.com. (Http://scienceblogs.com/thoughtfulanimal/2010/09/20/hints-of-moral-thinking-in-dog/)
264. Goldstein, M. H., Schwade, J. A., & Bornstein, M. H. (2009). The Value of Vocalizing: Five-Month-Old Infants Associate Their

Own Noncry Vocalizations With Responses From Caregivers. *Child Development, 80*(3), 636–644.

265. Gonzalez, M., Herrmann, H., Kertesz, J., & Vicsek, T. (2006). *Community Structure and Ethnic Preferences in School Friendship Networks.*

266. Gospic, K., Mohlin, E., Fransson, P., Petrovic, P., Johannesson, M., & Ingvar, M. (2011, 3 May). Limbic Justice - Amygdala Involvement in Immediate Rejection in the Ultimatum Game. *PLoS Biol, 9*(5).

267. Le Grand, R., Mondloch, C. J., Maurer, D., & Brent, H. P. (2001, 19 Apr). Early visual experience and face processing. *Nature, 410*(6831), 890–890. (Http://www.nature.com/nature/journal/v410/n6831/pdf/410890 a0.pdf)

268. Granovetter, M. (2003, 8 Aug). Ignorance, Knowledge, and Outcomes in a Small World. *Science, 301*(5634), 773–774. (Http://www.sciencemag.org/cgi/reprint/sci;301/5634/773.pdf)

269. Grant, K. (2001, 5 Dec). A Collaborative Research and Learning Methodology in SME's. Australian and New Zealand Marketing Academy Conference. Massey University, Auckland, NZ. (Http://smib.vuw.ac.nz:8081/WWW/ANZMAC2001/anzmac/AUTH ORS/pdfs/Grant1.pdf.)

270. Green, C. B., & Menaker, M. (2003, 18 Jul). Clocks on the Brain. *Science, 301*(5631), 319–320. (Http://www.sciencemag.org/cgi/reprint/sci;301/5631/319.pdf)

271. Greenberg, J. (2008). Understanding the Vital Human Quest for Self-Esteem. *Perspectives on Psychological Science, 3*(1).

272. Greenfield, P. M. (2009, 2 Jan). Technology and Informal Education: What Is Taught, What Is Learned. *Science, 323*(5910), 69–71. (Http://www.sciencemag.org/cgi/reprint/323/5910/69.pdf)

273. Greenspan, S. I., M.D., & Shanker, S. G., D. Phil. (2004). *The First Idea: How Symbols, Language, and Intelligence Evolved from Our Primate Ancestors to Modern Humans.* Da Capo Press. (Http://www.amazon.com/gp/product/0306814498?keywords=th e%20first%20idea&qid=1444753591&ref_=sr_1_1&sr=8-1)

274. Griffin, A. S., & West, S. A. (2003, 24 Oct). Kin Discrimination and the Benefit of Helping in Cooperatively Breeding Vertebrates. *Science, 302*(5645), 634–636. (Http://www.sciencemag.org/cgi/reprint/sci;302/5645/634.pdf)

275. Grodzinsky, Y., & Nelken, I. (2014, 28 Feb). The Neural Code That Makes Us Human. *Science, 343*(6174), 978–979. (Http://www.sciencemag.org/content/343/6174/978.full.pdf)

276. Grunspan, D., Eddy, S., Brownell, S., Wiggins, B., Crowe, A., & Goodreau, S. (2016, 10 Feb). Males Under-Estimate Academic Performance of Their Female Peers in Undergraduate Biology Classrooms. *PLoS ONE, 11*(2). (Http://journals.plos.org/plosone/article/asset?id=10.1371%2Fjournal.pone.0148405.PDF)

277. Guney, S., & Newell, B. (2013, 7 Jun). Fairness overrides reputation: The importance of fairness considerations in altruistic cooperation. *Frontiers in Human Neuroscience, 7.* (Http://www.frontiersin.org/Journal/DownloadFile.ashx?pdf=1&FileId=253957&articleId=47010&Version=1&ContentTypeId=21&FileName=fnhum-07-00252.pdf)

278. Gurerk, O., Irlenbusch, B., & Rockenbach, B. (2006, 7 Apr). The Competitive Advantage of Sanctioning Institutions. *Science, 312*(5770), 108–111. (Http://www.sciencemag.org/cgi/content/abstract/312/5770/108)

279. Ha, T., Overbeek, G., & Engels, R., C.M.E. Engels. (2010). Effects of Attractiveness and Social Status on Dating in Heterosexual Adolescents: An Experimental Study. *Archi Sex Behav, 39.*

280. Haidt, J. (2007, 18 May). The New Synthesis in Moral Psychology. *Science, 316*(5827), 998–1002. (Http://www.sciencemag.org/content/316/5827/998.full.pdf)

281. Halali, E., Bereby-Meyer, Y., & Ockenfels, A. (2013, 13 Jun). Is it all about the self? The effect of self-control depletion on ultimatum game proposers. *Frontiers in Human Neuroscience, 7.* (Http://www.frontiersin.org/Journal/DownloadFile.ashx?pdf=1&FileId=259454&articleId=48325&Version=1&ContentTypeId=21&FileName=fnhum-07-00240.pdf)

282. Halbert, D. (2009, 7 /Dev). Public lives and private communities: The terms of service agreement and life in virtual worlds. *First Monday, 14*(12). (Http://firstmonday.org/ojs/index.php/fm/article/view/2601/2405)

283. Hall, E. T. (1959). *The Silent Language.* Anchor.

284. Hall, E. T. (1966). *The Hidden Dimension.* Anchor.

285. Hall, E. T. (1976). *Beyond Culture.* Anchor.

286. Hall, L., Johansson, P., & Strandberg, T. (2012, 19 Sep). Lifting the Veil of Morality: Choice Blindness and Attitude Reversals on a Self-Transforming Survey. *PLoS ONE, 7*(9). (Http://www.plosone.org/article/fetchObjectAttachment.action;js essionid=5EE371615406C53003ECA1FBD3324E98?uri=info%3Ad oi%2F10.1371%2Fjournal.pone.0045457&representation=PDF)

287. Hallerberg, S., & Kantz H. (2008, 29 Jan). When are Extreme Events the better predictable, the larger they are? *arXiv:0801.4525, 1,* 14.

288. Harold Pashler, Mark McDaniel, Doug Rohrer, & Robert Bjork. (2008). Learning Styles: Concepts and Evidence. *Psychological Science in the Public Interest, 9*(3), 105–119. (Http://www.psychologicalscience.org/journals/pspi/PSPI_9_3.pdf http://dx.doi.org/10.1111/j.1539–6053.2009.01038.x)

289. Harris, L. T., & Fiske, S. T. (2006, 1 Oct). Dehumanizing the Lowest of the Low: Neuroimaging Responses to Extreme Out-Groups. *Psychological Science, 17*(10), 847–853. (Http://pss.sagepub.com/content/17/10/847.full.pdf+html)

290. Hasson, U., Nir, Y., Levy, I., Fuhrmann, G., & Malach, R. (2004, 12 Mar). Intersubject Synchronization of Cortical Activity During Natural Vision. *Science, 303*(5664), 1634–1640. (Http://www.sciencemag.org/cgi/reprint/sci;303/5664/1634.pdf)

291. Hauert, C., & Doebeli, M. (2004, 8 Apr). Spatial structure often inhibits the evolution of cooperation in the snowdrift game. *Nature, 428*(6983), 643–646. (Http://www.nature.com/nature/journal/v428/n6983/pdf/nature0 2360.pdf)

292. Hauert, C., Traulsen, A., Brandt, H., Nowak, M. A., & Sigmund, K. (2007, 29 Jun). Via Freedom to Coercion: The

Emergence of Costly Punishment. *Science, 316*(5833), 1905–1907.
(Http://www.sciencemag.org/content/316/5833/1905.full.pdf)
293. Haxby, J. V., Gobbini, M. I., Furey, M. L., Ishai, A., Schouten, J. L., & Pietrini, P. (2001, 28 Sep). Distributed and Overlapping Representations of Faces and Objects in Ventral Temporal Cortex. *Science, 293*(5539), 2425–2430.
(Http://www.sciencemag.org/cgi/reprint/sci;293/5539/2425.pdf)
294. Hayden, E. C. (2015, 24 Sep). Researchers wrestle with a privacy problem. *Nature, 525.*
(Http://www.nature.com/polopoly_fs/1.18396!/menu/main/topColumns/topLeftColumn/pdf/525440a.pdf)
295. Hazel Rose Markus, Y. U., Heather Omoregie. (2006, Feb). Going for the Gold - Models of Agency in Japanese and American Contexts. *Psychological Science, 17*(2), 103–112.
(Http://www3.interscience.wiley.com/cgi-bin/fulltext/118597327/PDFSTART)
296. Heinrichs, H. (2013, Dec). Sharing Economy: A Potential Pathway to Sustainability. *GAIA: Ecological Perspectives for Science & Society, 22*(4).
(Http://www.ingentaconnect.com/search/article?option1=tka&value1=%22sharing+economy%22&pageSize=10&index=2)
297. Heinsohn, R., & Packer, C. (1995, 1 Sep). Complex cooperative strategies in group-territorial African lions. *Science, 269*(5228), 1260–1262.
(Http://www.sciencemag.org/cgi/reprint/sci;269/5228/1260.pdf)
298. Helbing, D., Farkas, I., & Vicsek, T. (2000, 28 Sep). Simulating dynamical features of escape panic. *Nature, 407*(6803), 487–490.
(Http://www.nature.com/nature/journal/v407/n6803/pdf/407487a0.pdf)
299. Heller, S. B. (2014, 5 Dec). Summer jobs reduce violence among disadvantaged youth. *Science, 346*(6214), 1219–1223.
(Http://www.sciencemag.org/content/346/6214/1219.full.pdf)
300. Helmuth, L. (2002, 31 May). Redrawing the Brain's Map of the Body. *Science, 296*(5573), 1587a-1588.

(Http://www.sciencemag.org/cgi/reprint/sci;296/5573/1587a.pdf
)
301. Helmuth, L. (2003, 25 Apr). Fear and Trembling in the
Amygdala. *Science, 300*(5619), 568–569.
(Http://www.sciencemag.org/cgi/reprint/sci;300/5619/568.pdf)
302. Helmuth, L. (2002, 8 Nov). *Using Hands to See.*
ScienceNow.
(Http://sciencenow.sciencemag.org/cgi/content/full/2002/1108/4
)
303. Henkel, L. A. (2014, 1 Feb). Point-and-Shoot Memories: The
Influence of Taking Photos on Memory for a Museum Tour.
Psychological Science, 25(2), 396–402.
(Http://pss.sagepub.com/content/25/2/396.full.pdf+html)
304. Henrich, J., Ensminger, J., McElreath, R., Barr, A., Barrett,
C., Bolyanatz, A., et al. (2010, 19 Mar). Markets, Religion,
Community Size, and the Evolution of Fairness and Punishment.
Science, 327(5972), 1480–1484.
(Http://www.sciencemag.org/content/327/5972/1480.full.pdf)
305. Henrich, J., Heine, S. J., & Norenzayan, A. (2010). The
weirdest people in the world? *Behavioral and Brain
Sciences, 33,* 61–135.
(Http://s3.amazonaws.com/academia.edu.documents/790481/Ta
rget_and_commentaries.pdf?AWSAccessKeyId=0XGAZE282T5ZE
MSNEY02&Expires=1296742496&Signature=jGZrQOyKVdH6oX7B
%2BuDrj5oOSro%3D)
306. Henrich, J., McElreath, R., Barr, A., Ensminger, J., Barrett,
C., Bolyanatz, A., et al. (2006, 23 Jun). Costly Punishment Across
Human Societies. *Science, 312*(5781), 1767–1770.
(Http://www.sciencemag.org/content/312/5781/1767.full.pdf)
307. Henrich, J. (2004, 11 Mar). Animal behaviour
(communication arising): Inequity aversion in capuchins?
Nature, 428(6979), 139–139.
(Http://www.nature.com/nature/journal/v428/n6979/pdf/428139
a.pdf)
308. Henrich, J. (2006, 7 Apr). Cooperation, Punishment, and the
Evolution of Human Institutions. *Science, 312*(5770), 60–61.

309. Henrich, J. (2012, 26 Jan). Hunter-gatherer cooperation. *Nature, 481*(7382), 449–450.
(Http://www.nature.com/nature/journal/v481/n7382/pdf/481449 a.pdf)
310. Henrich, J. (2014, 9 May). Rice, Psychology, and Innovation. *Science, 344*(6184), 593–594.
(Http://www.sciencemag.org/content/344/6184/603.full.pdf)
311. Henry, P., & Hardin, C. D. (2006, 1 Oct). The Contact Hypothesis Revisited: Status Bias in the Reduction of Implicit Prejudice in the United States and Lebanon. *Psychological Science, 17*(10), 862–868.
(Http://pss.sagepub.com/content/17/10/862.full.pdf+html)
312. Herb, U. (2010, 1 Feb). Sociological implications of scientific publishing: Open access, science, society, democracy, and the digital divide. *First Monday, 15*(2).
(Http://firstmonday.org/ojs/index.php/fm/article/view/2599/2404)
313. Hinkle, V. (2008, Oct). Card-Sorting: What You Need to Know about Analyzing and Interpreting Card Sorting Results. *Usability News (Software Usability Research Laboratory (SURL) at Wichita State University), 10*(2).
(Http://www.surl.org/usabilitynews/102/pdf/Usability%20News% 20102%20-%20Hinkle.pdf)
314. Hodgson D. (2002). Three Tricks of Consciousness Qualia, Chunking and Selection. *Journal of Consciousness Studies, 9*(12), 65–88.
315. Hoff, K. (2010, 19 Mar). Fairness in Modern Society. *Science, 327*(5972), 1467–1468.
(Http://www.sciencemag.org/content/327/5972/1467.full.pdf)
316. Hofmann, W., Wisneski, D. C., Brandt, M. J., & Skitka, L. J. (2014, 12 Sep). Morality in everyday life. *Science, 345*(6202), 1340–1343.
(Http://www.sciencemag.org/content/345/6202/1340.full.pdf)
317. Holowka, S., & Petitto, L. A. (2002, 30 Aug). Left Hemisphere Cerebral Specialization for Babies While Babbling. *Science, 297*(5586).
(Http://www.sciencemag.org/cgi/reprint/sci;297/5586/1515.pdf)

318. Howard, P. N., & Kreiss, D. (2010, 6 Dec). Political parties and voter privacy: Australia, Canada, the United Kingdom, and United States in comparative perspective. *First Monday, 15*(12). (Http://firstmonday.org/htbin/cgiwrap/bin/ojs/index.php/fm/artic le/view/2975/2627)

319. Hulleman, C. S., & Harackiewicz, J. M. (2009, 4 Dec). Promoting Interest and Performance in High School Science Classes. *Science, 326*(5958), 1410–1412. (Http://www.sciencemag.org/cgi/reprint/sci;326/5958/1410.pdf)

320. Imhoff, R., & Banse, R. (2009, 1 Dec). Ongoing Victim Suffering Increases Prejudice: The Case of Secondary Anti-Semitism. *Psychological Science, 20*(12), 1443–1447. (Http://pss.sagepub.com/content/20/12/1443.full.pdf+html)

321. Immordino-Yang, M. H., McColl, A., Damasio, H., & Damasio, A. (2009, 20 Apr). Neural correlates of admiration and compassion. *Proceedings of the National Academy of Sciences, 106.* (Http://www.pnas.org/content/early/2009/04/17/0810363106.ful l.pdf+html)

322. Isbell, L. M. (2012, Oct). The Emotional Citizen. *APS Observer, 25.* (Http://www.psychologicalscience.org/index.php/publications/obs erver/2012/october-12/the-emotional-citizen.html#.UIfql2dB4xM)

323. Jacquet, J., Hauert, C., Traulsen, A., & Milinski, M. (2011, 1 Jun). Shame and honour drive cooperation. *Biology Letters, 7.* (Http://rsbl.royalsocietypublishing.org/content/early/2011/05/30/ rsbl.2011.0367.full.pdf+html)

324. Jaffe, E. (2011, Oct). The Complicated Psychology of Revenge. *APS Observer, 24.* (Http://www.psychologicalscience.org/index.php/publications/obs erver/2011/october-11/the-complicated-psychology-of-revenge.html)

325. Jansen, V. A. A., & van Baalen, M. (2006, 30 Mar). Altruism through beard chromodynamics. *Nature, 440,* 663–666. (Http://www.nature.com/nature/journal/v440/n7084/pdf/nature0 4387.pdf)

326. Janssen, M. A., Holahan, R., Lee, A., & Ostrom, E. (2010, 30 Apr). Lab Experiments for the Study of Social-Ecological Systems. *Science, 328*(5978), 613–617.
(Http://www.sciencemag.org/content/328/5978/613.full.pdf)
327. Jarvis, J. (2011, June). Privacy, Publicness, and the Web: A Manifesto. *ieee Spectrum.*
(Http://spectrum.ieee.org/telecom/internet/privacy-publicness-and-the-web-a-manifesto)
328. Jennings, J. H., Sparta, D. R., Stamatakis, A. M., Ung, R. L., Pleil, K. E., Kash, T. L., et al. (2013, 11 Apr). Distinct extended amygdala circuits for divergent motivational states.
Nature, 496(7444), 224–228.
(Http://www.nature.com/nature/journal/v496/n7444/pdf/nature1 2041.pdf)
329. Jeremy Ginges, & Scott Atran. (2009). What Motivates Participation in Violent Political Action. *Annals of the New York Academy of Sciences, 1167*(Values, Empathy, and Fairness across Social Barriers), 115–123.
(Http://www3.interscience.wiley.com/cgi-bin/fulltext/122466399/PDFSTART)
330. John, N. A. (2013, July). The Social Logics of Sharing. *The Communication Review, 16*(3), 113–131.
331. John Thomas Alderdice. (2009). Sacred Values. *Annals of the New York Academy of Sciences, 1167*(Values, Empathy, and Fairness across Social Barriers), 158–173.
(Http://www3.interscience.wiley.com/cgi-bin/fulltext/122466397/PDFSTART)
332. Jones, B. C., DeBruine, L. M., Little, A. C., Burriss, R. P., & Feinberg, D. R. (2007, 22 Mar). Social transmission of face preferences among humans. *Proceedings of the Royal Society B: Biological Sciences, 274*(1611), 899–903.
(Http://rspb.royalsocietypublishing.org/content/274/1611/899.full.pdf+html)
333. Joyce F. Benenson, H. M., Caitlin Fitzgerald. (2009, 5 Jan). Males' Greater Tolerance of Same-Sex Peers. *Psychological Science, 20*(2), 184–190.

(Http://www3.interscience.wiley.com/cgi-bin/fulltext/121615904/PDFSTART)
334. Kaminski, G., Dridi, S., Graff, C., & Gentaz, E. (2009, 7 Jul). Human ability to detect kinship in strangers' faces: Effects of the degree of relatedness. *Proceedings of the Royal Society B: Biological Sciences, 276*(1670), 3193–3200. (Http://rspb.royalsocietypublishing.org/content/276/1670/3193.full.pdf+html)
335. Kanai, R., Feilden, T., Firth, C., & Rees, G. (2011, 26 Apr). Political Orientations Are Correlated with Brain Structure in Young Adults. *Current biology: CB, 21*(8), 677–680. (Http://download.cell.com/current-biology/pdf/PIIS0960982211002892.pdf)
336. Kaul, V. (2012). Changing Paradigms of Media Landscape in the Digital Age. *Mass Communication and Journalism, 2*(2).
337. Kätsyri, J., Hari, R., Ravaja, N., & Nummenmaa, L. (2013, 13 Jun). Just watching the game ain't enough: Striatal fMRI reward responses to successes and failures in a video game during active and vicarious playing. *Frontiers in Human Neuroscience, 7.* (Http://www.frontiersin.org/Journal/DownloadFile.ashx?pdf=1&FileId=258811&articleId=51641&Version=1&ContentTypeId=21&FileName=fnhum-07-00278.pdf)
338. Kelley, T. C., & Hare, J. F. (2010). Pair-bonded humans conform to sexual stereotypes in web-based advertisements for extra-marital partners. *Evolutionary Psychology, 8*(4), 561–572. (Http://www.epjournal.net/filestore/EP085615722.pdf?utm_source=MadMimi&utm_medium=email&utm_content=November+2010+Newsletter&utm_campaign=November+2010+Newsletter&utm_term=Pair-bonded+humans+conform+to+sexual+stereotypes+in+web-based+advertisements+for+extra-marital+partners_)
339. Kemp, C., & Regier, T. (2012, 25 May). Kinship Categories Across Languages Reflect General Communicative Principles. *Science, 336*(6084), 1049–1054. (Http://www.sciencemag.org/content/336/6084/1049.full.pdf)

340. Kemp, M. (2009, 15 Oct). Art history's window onto the mind. *Nature, 461*(7266), 882–883.
(Http://www.nature.com/nature/journal/v461/n7266/pdf/461882
a.pdf)
341. Kepler, T. B., & Perelson, A. S. (1995, 29 Aug). Modeling and optimization of populations subject to time-dependent mutation. *Proceedings of the National Academy of Sciences of the United States of America, 92*(18), 8219–8223.
(Http://www.pnas.org/content/92/18/8219.full.pdf+html)
342. Kerth, G., Ebert, C., & Schmidtke, C. (2006, 7 Nov). Group decision making in fissionâ€"fusion societies: Evidence from two-field experiments in Bechstein's bats. *Proceedings of the Royal Society B: Biological Sciences, 273*(1602), 2785–2790.
(Http://rspb.royalsocietypublishing.org/content/273/1602/2785.f
ull.pdf+html)
343. Kerth, G., Perony, N., & Schweitzer, F. (2011, 22 Sep). Bats are able to maintain long-term social relationships despite the high fissionâ€"fusion dynamics of their groups. *Proceedings of the Royal Society B: Biological Sciences, 278*(1719), 2761–2767.
(Http://rspb.royalsocietypublishing.org/content/278/1719/2761.f
ull.pdf+html)
344. Kerth, G., & Reckard, K. (2003, 7 Mar). Information transfer about roosts in female Bechstein's bats: An experimental field study. *Proceedings of the Royal Society of London. Series B: Biological Sciences, 270*(1514).
(Http://rspb.royalsocietypublishing.org/content/270/1514/511.ful
l.pdf+html?sid=f3ace925–3288–48df-8dd2–5c76b34a57a5)
345. Khare, A., Santorelli, L. A., Strassmann, J. E., Queller, D. C., Kuspa, A., & Shaulsky, G. (2009, 15 Oct). Cheater-resistance is not futile. *Nature, 461*(7266), 980–982.
(Http://www.nature.com/nature/journal/v461/n7266/pdf/nature0
8472.pdf)
346. King, L. A., Hicks, J. A., & Abdelkhalik, J. (2009, 1 Dec). Death, Life, Scarcity, and Value: An Alternative Perspective on the Meaning of Death. *Psychological Science, 20*(12), 1459–1462.
(Http://pss.sagepub.com/content/20/12/1459.full.pdf+html)

347. Kinga, T.-K. (2001, Feb). Media and the Construction of the Ganguro Trend in Japan. *Journal of Mundane Behavior, 2*(1).
348. King-Casas, B., Tomlin, D., Anen, C., Camerer, C. F., Quartz, S. R., & Montague, P. R. (2005, 1 Apr). Getting to Know You: Reputation and Trust in a Two Person Economic Exchange. *Science, 308*(5718), 78–83. (Http://www.sciencemag.org/cgi/reprint/308/5718/78.pdf)
349. Kinsley, C. H., Madonia, L., Gifford, G. W., Tureski, K., Griffin, G. R., Lowry, C., et al. (1999, 11 Nov). Motherhood improves learning and memory. *Nature, 401*(6758), 137–138. (Http://www.nature.com/nature/journal/v402/n6758/pdf/402137 a0.pdf)
350. Kirchhoff, A. J. (2008, October). Digital preservation: Challenges and implementation. *Learned Publishing, 21*(4), 285–294.
351. Kirrane, E., & Carrabis, J. (2011, 28 Jan). *Joseph Carrabis - Fear Álainn.* Crepuscular Light. (Http://www.emerkirrane.com/2011/01/28/joseph-carrabis-fear-alainn/)
352. Klein, W. M., & Harris, P. R. (2009, 1 Dec). Self-Affirmation Enhances Attentional Bias Toward Threatening Components of a Persuasive Message. *Psychological Science, 20*(12), 1463–1467. (Http://pss.sagepub.com/content/20/12/1463.full.pdf+html)
353. Knight, J. (2003, 23 Jan). Meeting aims to find brain's benchmarks for beauty. *Nature, 421*(6921), 305–305. (Http://www.nature.com/nature/journal/v421/n6921/pdf/421305 b.pdf)
354. Koechlin, E., & Hyafil, A. (2007, 26 Oct). Anterior Prefrontal Function and the Limits of Human Decision-Making. *Science, 318*(5850), 594–598.
355. Koivisto, M., & Revonsuo, A. (2007, 1 Oct). How Meaning Shapes Seeing. *Psychological Science, 18*(10), 845–849. (Http://pss.sagepub.com/content/18/10/845.full.pdf+html)
356. Kouider, S., Stahlhut, C., Gelskov, S. V., Barbosa, L. S., Dutat, M., de Gardelle, V., et al. (2013, 19 Apr). A Neural Marker of Perceptual Consciousness in Infants. *Science, 340*(6130), 376–

380.
(Http://www.sciencemag.org/content/340/6130/376.full.pdf)
357. Kovacs, A. M., & Mehler, J. (2009, 31 Jul). Flexible Learning of Multiple Speech Structures in Bilingual Infants. *Science, 325*(5940), 611–612.
(Http://www.sciencemag.org/cgi/reprint/sci;325/5940/611.pdf)
358. Kozlovic, A. K. (2004). Lights! Camera! Sermon!: Additional Research Notes on Sacred Servant Categories Within the Popular Cinema. *Journal of Mundane Behavior, 5*(1).
359. Kozlowski, S. W., & Ilgen, D. R. (2006, Dec). Enhancing the Effectiveness of Work Groups and Teams. *Psychological Science in the Public Interest, 7*(3), 77–124.
(Http://www3.interscience.wiley.com/cgi-bin/fulltext/118600272/PDFSTART)
360. Krajbich, I., Camerer, C., Ledyard, J., & Rangel, A. (2009, 23 Oct). Using Neural Measures of Economic Value to Solve the Public Goods Free-Rider Problem. *Science, 326*(5952), 596–599.
(Http://www.sciencemag.org/cgi/reprint/sci;326/5952/596.pdf)
361. Kramer, A. D. I., Guillory, J. E., & Hancock, J. T. (2014, 17 Jun). Experimental evidence of massive-scale emotional contagion through social networks. *Proceedings of the National Academy of Sciences, 111*(24), 8788–8790.
362. Kreager, D. A., & Haynie, D. L. (2011, Oct). Dating and Drinking Diffusion in Adolescent Peer Networks. *American Sociological Review.*
(Http://www.asanet.org/images/journals/docs/pdf/asr/Oct11ASR Feature.pdf)
363. Kross, E. (2009). When the Self Becomes Other. *Annals of the New York Academy of Sciences, 1167*(Values, Empathy, and Fairness across Social Barriers), 35–40.
(Http://www3.interscience.wiley.com/cgi-bin/fulltext/122466387/PDFSTART)
364. Kuhn, S., Romanowski, A., Schilling, C., Lorenz, R., Morsen, C., Seiferth, N., et al. (2011, 15 Nov). The neural basis of video gaming. *Nature, 1.*
365. Kung, C. (2005, 4 Aug). A possible unifying principle for mechanosensation. *Nature, 436*(7051), 647–654.

(Http://www.nature.com/nature/journal/v436/n7051/pdf/nature0
3896.pdf)
366. Kurniawan, I., Seymour, B., Vlaev, I., Trommershäuser, J.,
Dolan, R., & Chater, N. (2010, 1 Jun). Pain Relativity in Motor
Control. *Psychological Science, 21*(6), 840–847.
(Http://pss.sagepub.com/content/21/6/840.full.pdf+html)
367. Kurzban, R., & Barrett, H. C. (2012, 2 Mar). Origins of
Cumulative Culture. *Science, 335*(6072), 1056–1057.
(Http://www.sciencemag.org/content/335/6072/1056.full.pdf)
368. Kuzmanovic, B., Jefferson, A., Bente, G., & Vogeley, K.
(2013, 11 Jun). Affective and motivational influences in person
perception. *Frontiers in Human Neuroscience, 7.*
(Http://www.frontiersin.org/Journal/DownloadFile.ashx?pdf=1&Fil
eId=256145&articleId=48408&Version=1&ContentTypeId=21&Fil
eName=fnhum-07-00266.pdf)
369. Lacetera, N., Macis, M., & Slonim, R. (2013, 24 May).
Economic Rewards to Motivate Blood Donations.
Science, 340(6135), 927–928.
(Http://www.sciencemag.org/content/340/6135/927.full.pdf)
370. Lang, A., Park, B., Sanders-Jackson, A. N., Wilson, B. D., &
Wang, S. (2007). Cognition and Emotion in TV Message
Processing: How Valence, Arousing Content, Structural
Complexity, and Information Density Affect the Availability of
Cognitive Resources. *Media Psychology, 10,* 317–338.
371. Laughlin, B. (2001, Jul). Satisfaction Survey by Web or by
Paper? A Case Study at a Fortune 500 Company. *Usability News
(Software Usability Research Laboratory (SURL) at Wichita State
University), 3*(2).
372. Layard, R. (2010, 19 Jan). Measuring Subjective Well-Being.
Science, 327(5965), 534–535.
(Http://www.sciencemag.org/cgi/reprint/sci;327/5965/534.pdf)
373. Lee, F. S., Heimer, H., Giedd, J. N., Lein, E. S., Aestan, N.,
Weinberger, D. R., et al. (2014, 31 Oct). Adolescent mental
health - Opportunity and obligation. *Science, 346*(6209), 547–
549.
(Http://www.sciencemag.org/content/346/6209/547.full.pdf)

374. Leighton, J., Bird, G., Orsini, C., & Heyes, C. (2010, Nov). Social attitudes modulate automatic imitation. *Journal of Experimental Social Psychology, 46*(6), 905–910. (Http://www.sciencedirect.com/science?_ob=MImg&_imagekey= B6WJB-50J9H8D-1– 5&_cdi=6874&_user=10&_pii=S0022103110001526&_origin=sea rch&_coverDate=11%2F30%2F2010&_sk=999539993&view=c&w chp=dGLbVlb- zSkzS&md5=2cb962e997fb4bcd7c7842c5c92c095f&ie=/sdarticle. pdf)

375. Lenz, K., & Fox, D. (2008, Oct). Examining the Critical User Interface Components of First-Person Shooter (FPS) Games. *Usability News (Software Usability Research Laboratory (SURL) at Wichita State University), 10*(2). (Http://www.surl.org/usabilitynews/102/pdf/Usability%20News% 20102%20-%20Lenz.pdf)

376. Lessig, L. (2008). *Remix: Making Art and Commerce Thrive in the Hybrid Economy.* Pengruin Press HC. (Http://www.amazon.com/Remix-Making-Commerce-Thrive- Economy/dp/1594201722/ref=sr_1_1/176–6557383– 1089838?s=books&ie=UTF8&qid=1420339303&sr=1– 1&keywords=9781594201721)

377. Lettvin, J. Y., Maturana, H. R., McCulloch, W. S., & Pitts, W. H. (1968). What the Frog's Eye Tells the Frog's Brain. *Proc. Inst. Radio Engr., 47,* 1940–1951. (Http://jerome.lettvin.info/lettvin/Jerome/WhatTheFrogsEyeTellsT heFrogsBrain.pdf)

378. Levav, J., & Argo, J. J. (2010, 1 Jun). Physical Contact and Financial Risk Taking. *Psychological Science, 21*(6), 804–810. (Http://pss.sagepub.com/content/21/6/804.full.pdf+html)

379. Levine, J. A., Weisell, R., Chevassus, S., Martinez, C. D., Burlingame, B., & Coward, W. A. (2001, 26 Oct). The Work Burden of Women. *Science, 294*(5543), 812. (Http://www.sciencemag.org/cgi/reprint/sci;294/5543/812.pdf)

380. Levinson, S. C. (2012, 25 May). Kinship and Human Thought. *Science, 336*(6084), 988–989. (Http://www.sciencemag.org/content/336/6084/988.full.pdf)

381. Lewis, K., Gonzalez, M., & Kaufman, J. (2012, 3 Jan). Social selection and peer influence in an online social network. *Proceedings of the National Academy of Sciences, 109*(1), 68–72.
382. Lilach Nir, & Ariel Knafo. (2009). Reason within Passion. *Annals of the New York Academy of Sciences, 1167*(Values, Empathy, and Fairness across Social Barriers), 146–157. (Http://www3.interscience.wiley.com/cgi-bin/fulltext/122466382/PDFSTART)
383. Little, A. C., DeBruine, L. M., & Jones, B. C. (2011, 7 Jul). Exposure to visual cues of pathogen contagion changes preferences for masculinity and symmetry in opposite-sex faces. *Proceedings of the Royal Society B: Biological Sciences, 278*(1714), 2032–2039. (Http://rspb.royalsocietypublishing.org/content/278/1714/2032.full.pdf+html)
384. Lleras, A., & Moore, C. M. (2006, 1 Oct). What You See Is What You Get: Functional Equivalence of a Perceptually Filled-In Surface and a Physically Presented Stimulus. *Psychological Science, 17*(10), 876–881. (Http://pss.sagepub.com/content/17/10/876.full.pdf+html)
385. Lopez, B. H. (1978). *Of Wolves and Men.* New York: Charles Scribner's Sons.
386. Lopez, B. H. (2001). *Arctic Dreams.* New York: Vintage.
387. Macapagal, K., Janssen, E., Fridberg, D., Finn, P., & Heiman, J. (2011-10-01). The Effects of Impulsivity, Sexual Arousability, and Abstract Intellectual Ability on Men's and Women's Go/No-Go Task Performance. *Archives of Sexual Behavior, 40*(5), 995–1006. Springer Netherlands.
388. MacLean, K. A., Ferrer, E., Aichele, S. R., Bridwell, D. A., Zanesco, A. P., Jacobs, T. L., et al. (2010, 1 Jun). Intensive Meditation Training Improves Perceptual Discrimination and Sustained Attention. *Psychological Science, 21*(6), 829–839. (Http://pss.sagepub.com/content/21/6/829.full.pdf+html)
389. Magee. Joe C. (2009, 24 Jul). Seeing power in action: The roles of deliberation, implementation, and action in inferences of power. *Journal of Experimental Social Psychology, 45,* 1–14.

390. Mahon, B. Z., Schwarzbach, J., & Caramazza, A. (2010, 1 Jun). The Representation of Tools in Left Parietal Cortex Is Independent of Visual Experience. *Psychological Science, 21*(6), 764–771. (Http://pss.sagepub.com/content/21/6/764.full.pdf+html)

391. Mai, J.-E. (2010). Classification in a social world: Bias and trust. *Journal of Documentation, 66*(5), 627–642.

392. Malach, R., Reppas, J. B., Benson, R. R., Kwong, K. K., Jiang, H., Kennedy, W. A., et al. (1995, 29 Aug). Object-related activity revealed by functional magnetic resonance imaging in human occipital cortex. *Proceedings of the National Academy of Sciences of the United States of America, 92*(18), 8135–8139. (Http://www.pnas.org/content/92/18/8135.full.pdf+html)

393. Marcus, G. F., Vijayan, S., Bandi Rao, S., & Vishton, P. M. (1999, 1 Jan). Rule Learning by Seven-Month-Old Infants. *Science, 283*(5398), 77–80. (Http://www.sciencemag.org/cgi/reprint/sci;283/5398/77.pdf)

394. Mark Van Vugt. (2009). Sex Differences in Intergroup Competition, Aggression, and Warfare. *Annals of the New York Academy of Sciences, 1167*(Values, Empathy, and Fairness across Social Barriers), 124–134. (Http://www3.interscience.wiley.com/cgi-bin/fulltext/122466380/PDFSTART)

395. Martin, J. L. (2009). *Social Structures.* Princeton, NJ: Princeton University Press.

396. Martinez, G. M., & Abma, J. C. (2015). *Sexual Activity, Contraceptive Use, and Childbearing of Teenagers Aged 15–19 in the United States.* CDC: CDC. (Http://www.cdc.gov/nchs/data/databriefs/db209.pdf)

397. Masum, H., & Zhang, Y.-C. (2008). Manifesto for the Reputation Society. *First Monday.*

398. Matsumoto, K., Suzuki, W., & Tanaka, K. (2003, 11 Jul). Neuronal Correlates of Goal-Based Motor Selection in the Prefrontal Cortex. *Science, 301*(5630), 229–232. (Http://www.sciencemag.org/cgi/reprint/sci;301/5630/229.pdf)

399. McCabe, K., Houser, D., Ryan, L., Smith, V., & Trouard, T. (2001, 25 Sep). A functional imaging study of cooperation in two-

person reciprocal exchange. *Proceedings of the National Academy of Sciences of the United States of America, 98*(20), 11832–11835.
(Http://www.pnas.org/content/98/20/11832.full.pdf+html)
400. McMahon, J. A. (2000). Perceptual Principles as the Basis for Genuine Judgments of Beauty. *Journal of Consciousness Studies, 7*(8–9), 29–35.
(Http://www.ingentaconnect.com/content/imp/jcs/2000/0000000 7/F0020008/1039)
401. McMains, S. A., & Somers, D. C. (2005, 12 Oct). Processing Efficiency of Divided Spatial Attention Mechanisms in Human Visual Cortex. *Journal of Neuroscience, 25*(41), 9444–9448.
(Http://www.jneurosci.org/cgi/reprint/25/41/9444)
402. Mears, D. P., &. (2002, Jun). The Ubiquity, Functions, and Contexts of Bullshitting*. *Journal of Mundane Behavior, 3*(2).
403. Meixner, J. B., & Rosenfeld, J. P. (2014, 1 Nov). Detecting Knowledge of Incidentally Acquired, Real-World Memories Using a P300-Based Concealed-Information Test. *Psychological Science, 25*(11), 1994–2005.
404. Mejia, N. N. (2008). Viral Marketing.
405. Melis, A. P., Hare, B., & Tomasello, M. (2006, 3 March). Chimpanzees Recruit the Best Collaborators. *Science, 311,* 1297–1300.
406. Meskauskas, J. (2005, 14 July). *Word of Mouth - The Little Bug that Could.* IMediaConnection.
(Www.imediaconnection.com/content/6322.asp)
407. Mesterton-Gibbons, M., & Adams, E. S. (2002, 13 Dec). The Economics of Animal Cooperation. *Science, 298*(5601), 2146–2147.
(Http://www.sciencemag.org/cgi/reprint/sci;298/5601/2146.pdf)
408. Meyer, K. (2012, 27 Jan). Another Remembered Present. *Science, 335*(6067), 415–416.
(Http://www.sciencemag.org/content/335/6067/415.full.pdf)
409. Michael R. Waldmann, Y. H., Aaron P. Blaisdell. (2006). Beyond the Information Given: Causal Models in Learning and Reasoning. *Current Directions in Psychological Science, 15*(6), 307–311.

(Http://www3.interscience.wiley.com/cgi-bin/fulltext/118584120/PDFSTART)
410. Miles, L. K., Nind, L. K., Henderson, Z., & Macrae, C. N. (2010, Mar). Moving memories: Behavioral synchrony and memory for self and others. *Journal of Experimental Social Psychology, 46*(2), 457–460.
(Http://www.sciencedirect.com/science?_ob=MImg&_imagekey=B6WJB-4XY4N64-2-9&_cdi=6874&_user=10&_pii=S0022103109003126&_origin=search&_coverDate=03%2F31%2F2010&_sk=999539997&view=c&wchp=dGLzVtz-zSkWA&md5=797caa9a2c9f3575b4dceb78bf675394&ie=/sdarticle.pdf)
411. Miliniski, M., Semmann, D., & Krambeck, H.-J. (2002, 24 January). Reputation helps solve the 'tragedy of the commons.' *Nature, 415,* 424–426.
412. Miller, G. (2007, 7 Sep). All Together Now--Pull! *Science, 317*(5843), 1338–1340.
(Http://www.sciencemag.org/cgi/reprint/317/5843/1338.pdf)
413. Miller, J. (1991). The flanker compatibility effect as a function of visual angle, attentional focus,visual transients, and perceptual load: A search for boundary conditions. *Perception and Psychophysics, 49,* 270–288.
(Http://www.psychonomic.org/search/view.cgi?id=5499)
414. Millikan, R. G. (1998). A common structure for concepts of individuals, stuffs, and real kinds: More Mama, more milk, and more mouse. *Behavioral and Brain Sciences, 21*(01), 55–65.
415. Mitchell, J. F., Stoner, G. R., & Reynolds, J. H. (2004, 27 May). Object-based attention determines dominance in binocular rivalry. *Nature, 429*(6990), 410–413.
(Http://www.nature.com/nature/journal/v429/n6990/pdf/nature02584.pdf)
416. Mitchell, M. (2010). Understanding Meaning.
417. Mitchell, T. M. (2009, 18 Dec). Mining Our Reality. *Science, 326*(5960), 1644–1645.
(Http://www.sciencemag.org/cgi/reprint/326/5960/1644.pdf)

418. Mobbs, D., Yu, R., Meyer, M., Passamonti, L., Seymour, B., Calder, A. J., et al. (2009, 15 May). A Key Role for Similarity in Vicarious Reward. *Science, 324*(5929).
(Http://www.sciencemag.org/cgi/reprint/324/5929/900.pdf)
419. Morell, V. (1995, 1 Sep). Cowardly lions confound cooperation theory. *Science, 269*(5228), 1216–1217.
(Http://www.sciencemag.org/cgi/reprint/sci;269/5228/1216.pdf)
420. Morewedge, C. K., Huh, Y. E., & Vosgerau, J. (2010, 10 Dec). Thought for Food: Imagined Consumption Reduces Actual Consumption. *Science, 330*(6010), 1530–1533.
(Http://www.sciencemag.org/content/330/6010/1530.full.pdf)
421. Mui, C. (2011, 17 Oct). *Five Dangerous Lessons to Learn from Steve Jobs.* Forbes.
(Http://www.forbes.com/sites/chunkamui/2011/10/17/five-dangerous-lessons-to-learn-from-steve-jobs/)
422. Nabeth, T. (2005). *Understanding the Identity Concept in the Context of Digital Social Environments.* INSEAD CALT: INSEAD.
423. Nadine Forget-Dubois, G. D., Jean-Pascal Lemelin. (2009). Early Child Language Mediates the Relation Between Home Environment and School Readiness. *Child Development, 80*(3), 736–749.
424. Namy, L. L., & Waxman, S. R. (2000, 1 Jan). Naming and Exclaiming: Infants' Sensitivity to Naming Contexts. *Journal of Cognitive Development, 1*(4), 405–428.
(Http://www.informaworld.com/smpp/ftinterface~content=a785035641~fulltext=713240930)
425. Nate Kornell, & Robert A. Bjork. (2008, 10 Jun). Learning Concepts and Categories: Is Spacing the "Enemy of Induction?". *Psychological Science, 19*(6), 585–592.
(Http://www3.interscience.wiley.com/cgi-bin/fulltext/120086988/PDFSTART
http://dx.doi.org/10.1111/j.1467-9280.2008.02127.x)
426. Nelissen, K., Luppino, G., Vanduffel, W., Rizzolatti, G., & Orban, G. A. (2005, 14 Oct). Observing Others: Multiple Action Representation in the Frontal Lobe. *Science, 310*(5746), 332–

336.
(Http://www.sciencemag.org/content/310/5746/332.full.pdf)
427. Newman, A. L. (2015, 30 Jan). What the 'right to be forgotten' means for privacy in a digital age.
Science, 347(6221), 507–508.
428. Niwa, M., Jaaro-Peled, H., Tankou, S., Seshadri, S., Hikida, T., Matsumoto, Y., et al. (2013, 18 Jan). Adolescent Stress-Induced Epigenetic Control of Dopaminergic Neurons via Glucocorticoids. *Science, 339*(6117), 335–339.
(Http://www.sciencemag.org/content/339/6117/335.full.pdf)
429. Nowak, M. A., Komarova, N. L., & Niyogi, P. (2002, 6 June). Computational and evolutionary aspects of language.
Nature, 417(6889), 611–617.
(Http://www.nature.com/nature/journal/v417/n6889/pdf/nature00771.pdf)
430. Nowak, M. A., Page, K. M., & Sigmund, K. (2000, 8 Sept). Fairness versus Reason in the Ultimatum Game.
Science, 289, 1773–1775.
431. Nowak, M. A., Sasaki, A., Taylor, C., & Fudenberg, D. (2004, 8 Apr). Emergence of cooperation and evolutionary stability in finite populations. *Nature, 428*(6983), 646–650.
(Http://www.nature.com/nature/journal/v428/n6983/pdf/nature02414.pdf)
432. Nowak, M. A., & Sigmund, K. (2004, 6 Feb). Evolutionary Dynamics of Biological Games. *Science, 303*(5659), 793–799.
(Http://www.sciencemag.org/cgi/reprint/303/5659/793.pdf)
433. Nowak, M. A., & Sigmund, K. (2005, 27 Oct). Evolution of indirect reciprocity. *Nature, 437*(7063), 1291–1298.
(Http://www.nature.com/nature/journal/v437/n7063/pdf/nature04131.pdf)
434. Nowak, M. A. (2008, 4 Dec). Generosity: A winner's advice. *Nature, 456*(7222), 579–579.
(Http://www.nature.com/nature/journal/v456/n7222/full/456579a.html)
435. Offer, S., & Schneider, B. (2011, Dec). Revisiting the Gender Gap in Time-Use Patterns: Multitasking and Well-Being among Mothers and Fathers in Dual-Earner Families. *American*

Sociological Review.
(Http://www.asanet.org/images/journals/docs/pdf/asr/Dec11ASR
Feature.pdf)
436. Ohbayashi, M., Ohki, K., & Miyashita, Y. (2003, 11 Aug).
Conversion of Working Memory to Motor Sequence in the Monkey
Premotor Cortex. *Science, 301*(5630), 233–236.
(Http://www.sciencemag.org/cgi/reprint/301/5630/233.pdf)
437. Ohman, A. (2005, 29 Jul). Conditioned Fear of a Face: A
Prelude to Ethnic Enmity? *Science, 309*(5735), 711–713.
(Http://www.sciencemag.org/cgi/reprint/sci;309/5735/711.pdf)
438. Ohtsuki, H., Hauert, C., Lieberman, E., & Nowak, M. A.
(2006, 25 May). A simple rule for the evolution of cooperation on
graphs and social networks. *Nature, 441*(7092), 502–505.
439. Ohtsuki, H., Iwasa, Y., & Nowak, M. A. (2009, 1 Jan).
Indirect reciprocity provides only a narrow margin of efficiency for
costly punishment. *Nature, 457*(7225), 79–82.
(Http://www.nature.com/nature/journal/v457/n7225/suppinfo/na
ture07601_S1.html)
440. Olson, K. R., Banaji, M. R., Dweck, C. S., & Spelke, E. S.
(2006, 1 Oct). Children's Biased Evaluations of Lucky Versus
Unlucky People and Their Social Groups. *Psychological
Science, 17*(10), 845–846.
(Http://pss.sagepub.com/content/17/10/845.full.pdf+html)
441. Olsson, A., Ebert, J. P., Banaji, M. R., & Phelps, E. A. (2005,
29 Jul). The Role of Social Groups in the Persistence of Learned
Fear. *Science, 309*(5735), 785–787.
(Http://www.sciencemag.org/cgi/reprint/309/5735/785.pdf)
442. On One's Own Time. (2016, Jul/Aug). *APS Observer, 29,* 6.
(Http://www.psychologicalscience.org/index.php/publications/obs
erver/2016/july-august-16/on-ones-own-time.html)
443. *Online Video Viewing Passes 50% of Total US Population.*
(2011, 8 Dec). EMarketer.
(Http://www.emarketer.com/Article.aspx?R=1008724)
444. Oswald, A. J., & Wu, S. (2010, 29 Jan). Objective
Confirmation of Subjective Measures of Human Well-Being:
Evidence from the U.S.A. *Science, 327*(5965), 576–579.
(Http://www.sciencemag.org/cgi/reprint/327/5965/576.pdf)

445. Otamendi, R. D., Carrabis, J., & Carrabis, S. (2009). *Predicting Age & Gender Online*. Brussels, Belgium: NextStage Analytics.

446. Otamendi, R. D. (2009, 22 Oct). *NextStage Announcements at eMetrics Marketing Optimization Summit Washington DC*. NextStage Analytics. (Http://makingmarketingactionable.com/2009/10/22/nextstage-announcements-at-emetrics-marketing-optimization-summit-washington-dc/?CFID=148013&CFTOKEN=70102829)

447. Otamendi, R. D. (2009, 24 Nov). *NextStage Rich PersonaeTM classification*. NextStage Analytics. (Http://makingmarketingactionable.com/2009/11/24/nextstage-rich-personaetm-classification/comment-page-1/)

448. Oury, C., & Poll, R. (2013). Counting the uncountable: Statistics for web archives. *Performance Measurement and Metrics, 14*(2), 132–141.

449. Owens, J., Shaikh, A. D., & Chaparro, B. (2010, Nov). Creatures of Habit or Convenience? Users Still Use Browser Bookmarks and Email to Save Information. *Usability News (Software Usability Research Laboratory (SURL) at Wichita State University), 12*(2). (Http://www.surl.org/usabilitynews/122/pdf/Usability%20News%20122%20-%20Owens.pdf)

450. Papadopoulos, F., Kitsak, M., Serrano, M. A., Boguna, M., & Krioukov, D. (2012, 27 Sep). Popularity versus similarity in growing networks. *Nature, 489*(7417), 537–540. (Http://www.nature.com/nature/journal/v489/n7417/pdf/nature11459.pdf)

451. Parasuraman, R., & Galster, S. (2013, 12 Jun). Sensing, assessing, and augmenting threat detection: Behavioral, neuroimaging, and brain stimulation evidence for the critical role of attention. *Frontiers in Human Neuroscience, 7*. (Http://www.frontiersin.org/Journal/DownloadFile.ashx?pdf=1&FileId=257889&articleId=52500&Version=1&ContentTypeId=21&FileName=fnhum-07–00273.pdf)

452. Pascual-Leone, A. (2001, Jun). The Brain That Plays Music and Is Changed by It. *Annals of the New York Academy of*

Sciences, 930(1), 315–329.
(Http://onlinelibrary.wiley.com/doi/10.1111/j.1749–
6632.2001.tb05741.x/pdf)
453. Pasquale, F. (2015). *The Black Box Society: The Secret
Algorithms that Control Money and Information.* Harvard
University Press.
454. Paterson, S. J., Brown, J. H., Gs&ouml, dl, M. K., Johnson,
M. H., & Karmiloff-Smith, A. (1999, 17 Dec). Cognitive Modularity
and Genetic Disorders. *Science, 286*(5448), 2355–2358.
(Http://www.sciencemag.org/cgi/reprint/286/5448/2355.pdf)
455. Paul E. Dux, V. C. (2005, Oct). The Meaning of the Mask
Matters. *Psychological Science, 16*(10), 775–779.
(Http://www3.interscience.wiley.com/cgi-
bin/fulltext/118661659/PDFSTART)
456. Paul Slovic, E. P. (2006). Risk Perception and Affect. *Current
Directions in Psychological Science, 15*(6), 322–325.
(Http://www3.interscience.wiley.com/cgi-
bin/fulltext/118584123/PDFSTART)
457. Payne, B. K. (2006). Weapon Bias: Split-Second Decisions
and Unintended Stereotyping. *Current Directions in Psychological
Science, 15*(6), 287–291.
(Http://www3.interscience.wiley.com/cgi-
bin/fulltext/118584116/PDFSTART)
458. Paynter, J., & Satitkit, S. (2002, 3 Dec). User Perceptions of
Travel Industry Websites. ANZMAC.
(Http://smib.vuw.ac.nz:8081/WWW/ANZMAC2001/anzmac/AUTH
ORS/pdfs/Paynter.pdf)
459. Pearson, H. (2015, 22 Oct). The lab that knows where your
time really goes. *Nature, 526.*
(Http://www.nature.com/polopoly_fs/1.18609!/menu/main/topCo
lumns/topLeftColumn/pdf/526492a.pdf)
460. Pennisi, E. (2009, 4 Sep). On the Origin of Cooperation.
Science, 325(5945), 1196–1199.
(Http://www.sciencemag.org/cgi/reprint/325/5945/1196.pdf)
461. Persson, A. (2001, Oct). Intimacy Among Strangers: On
mobile telephone calls in public places. *Journal of Mundane
Behavior, 2*(3).

462. Peshek, D., Semmaknejad, N., Hoffman, D., & Foley, P. (2011). Preliminary Evidence that the Limbal Ring Influences Facial Attractiveness. *Evolutionary Psychology, 9*(2), 137–146. (Http://www.epjournal.net/filestore/EP09137146.pdf?utm_source =MadMimi&utm_medium=email&utm_content=May+2011+Newsl etter&utm_campaign=May+2011+Newsletter&utm_term=Prelimi nary+evidence+that+the+limbal+ring+influences+facial+attracti veness_)
463. Pessoa, L. (2004, 12 Mar). Seeing the World in the Same Way. *Science, 303*(5664), 1617–1618. (Http://www.sciencemag.org/cgi/reprint/303/5664/1617.pdf)
464. Peter, J., & Valkenburg, P. (2007–03–01). Adolescents' Exposure to a Sexualized Media Environment and Their Notions of Women as Sex Objects. *Sex Roles, 56*(5), 381–395. Springer Netherlands.
465. Peter, J., & Valkenburg, P. (2011–10–01). The Use of Sexually Explicit Internet Material and Its Antecedents: A Longitudinal Comparison of Adolescents and Adults. *Archives of Sexual Behavior, 40*(5), 1015–1025. Springer Netherlands.
466. Phillips, M. L. (2009, 12 Mar). Of owls, larks and alarm clocks. *Nature, 458*(7235), 142–144. (Http://www.nature.com/news/2009/090311/pdf/458142a.pdf)
467. Poulin, M. (2012, Dec). Our Genes Want Us to Be Altruists. *APS Observer, 25.* (Http://www.psychologicalscience.org/index.php/publications/obs erver/2012/december-12/our-genes-want-us-to-be- altruists.html)
468. Powell, A., Shennan, S., & Thomas, M. G. (2009, 5 Jun). Late Pleistocene Demography and the Appearance of Modern Human Behavior. *Science, 324*(5932), 1298–1301. (Http://www.sciencemag.org/cgi/reprint/324/5932/1298.pdf)
469. Powell, R. M. Using Traditional Gender Norms to Expand Gender: A Qualitative Study of Old Time Dance Communities. *Journal of Mundane Behavior, 3*(1).
470. Prut, Y., & Fetz, E. E. (1999, 7 Oct). Primate spinal interneurons show pre-movement instructed delay activity. *Nature, 401*(6753), 590–594.

(Http://www.nature.com/nature/journal/v401/n6753/pdf/401590
a0.pdf)
471. Puce, A., McNeely, M. E., Berrebi, M., Thompson, J. C.,
Hardee, J. E., & Brefczynski-Lewis, J. (2013, 14 Jun). Multiple
faces elicit augmented neural activity. *Frontiers in Human
Neuroscience, 7.*
(Http://www.frontiersin.org/Journal/DownloadFile.ashx?pdf=1&Fil
eId=260526&articleId=32917&Version=1&ContentTypeId=21&Fil
eName=fnhum-07-00282.pdf)
472. Putterman, L. (2010, 30 Apr). Cooperation and Punishment.
Science, 328(5978), 578–579.
(Http://www.sciencemag.org/content/328/5978/578.full.pdf)
473. Raihani, N. J., Grutter, A. S., & Bshary, R. (2010/1/8).
Punishers Benefit From Third-Party Punishment in Fish.
Science, 327(5962).
474. Ramachandran, V., & Hirstein, W. (1999). The Science of Art
- A Neurological Theory of Aesthetic Experience. *Journal of
Consciousness Studies, 6*(6–7), 15–51.
(Http://www.ingentaconnect.com/content/imp/jcs/1999/0000000
6/F0020006/949)
475. Ramsden, S., Richardson, F. M., Josse, G., Thomas, M. S. C.,
Ellis, C., Shakeshaft, C., et al. (2011, 3 Nov). Verbal and non-
verbal intelligence changes in the teenage brain.
Nature, 479(7371), 113–116.
(Http://www.nature.com/nature/journal/v479/n7371/pdf/nature1
0514.pdf)
476. Ran R. Hassin, Melissa J. Ferguson, Rasha Kardosh,
Shanette C. Porter, Travis J. Carter, & Veronika Dudareva.
(2009). Precis of Implicit Nationalism. *Annals of the New York
Academy of Sciences, 1167*(Values, Empathy, and Fairness across
Social Barriers), 135–145.
(Http://www3.interscience.wiley.com/cgi-
bin/fulltext/122466395/PDFSTART)
477. Rand, D. G., Dreber, A., Ellingsen, T., Fudenberg, D., &
Nowak, M. A. (2009, 4 Sep). Positive Interactions Promote Public
Cooperation. *Science, 325*(5945), 1272–1275.
(Http://www.sciencemag.org/cgi/reprint/sci;325/5945/1272.pdf)

478. Rand, D. G., Nowak, M. A., Fowler, J. H., & Christakis, N. A. (2014, 2 Dec). Static network structure can stabilize human cooperation. *Proceedings of the National Academy of Sciences, 111*(48), 17093–17098. (Http://www.pnas.org/content/111/48/17093.full.pdf)
479. Rawlins, B. L. (2007, 29 Oct). *Trust and PR Practice.* Institute for Public Relations. (Http://www.instituteforpr.org/topics/trust-and-pr-practice/)
480. Raynes-Goldie, K. (2010, 4 Jan). Aliases, Creeping, and wall cleaning, Understanding privacy in the age of Facebook. *First Monday, 15*(1). (Http://firstmonday.org/ojs/index.php/fm/article/view/2775/2432)
481. Reber, A. S. (1993). *Implicit Learning and Tacit Knowledge. An Essay on the Cognitive Unconscious.* Oxford Psychology Series. Oxford: Oxford University Press.
482. Regier, T., Kay, P., & Cook, R. S. (2005, 7 June). Focal Colors Are Universal After All. *Proceedings of the National Academy of Sciences of the United States of America, 102*(23), 8386–8391. (Http://www.pnas.org/content/102/23/8386.full.pdf+html)
483. Reich, E. S. (2011, 11 May). Best Face Forward. *Nature, 473,* 138–139. (Http://www.nature.com/news/2011/110511/pdf/473138a.pdf)
484. Reinout W. Wiers, A. W. S. (2006). Implicit Cognition and Addiction. *Current Directions in Psychological Science, 15*(6), 292–296. (Http://www3.interscience.wiley.com/cgi-bin/fulltext/118584117/PDFSTART)
485. Rellini, A., & Meston, C. (2011–04–01). Sexual Self-Schemas, Sexual Dysfunction, and the Sexual Responses of Women with a History of Childhood Sexual Abuse. *Archives of Sexual Behavior, 40*(2), 351–362. Springer Netherlands.
486. Ren, J., Wang, W.-X., & Qi, F. (2006). Randomness enhances cooperation: A resonance type phenomenon in evolutionary games. *Physical Review E, 75*(4), 4. (Http://arxiv.org/pdf/cond-mat/0607457v2)

487. Rentfrow, P. J., & Gosling, S. D. (2006, 1 Mar). Message in a Ballad. *Psychological Science, 17*(3), 236–242. (Http://pss.sagepub.com/content/17/3/236.full.pdf+html)
488. Richardson, D. S., Komdeur, J., & Burke, T. (2003, 10 Apr). Avian behaviour: Altruism and infidelity among warblers. *Nature, 422*(6932), 580–580. (Http://www.nature.com/nature/journal/v422/n6932/pdf/422580 a.pdf)
489. Richerson, P. (2013, 21 Nov). Group size determines cultural complexity. *Nature, 503*(7476), 351–352. (Http://www.nature.com/nature/journal/v503/n7476/pdf/nature1 2708.pdf)
490. Richmond, B. J., Liu, Z., & Shidara, M. (2003, 11 Jul). Predicting Future Rewards. *Science, 301*(5630), 179–180. (Http://www.sciencemag.org/cgi/reprint/sci;301/5630/179.pdf)
491. Rickles, D., & Kon, M. (2014). Interdisciplinary perspectives on the flow of time. *Annals of the New York Academy of Sciences, 1326*(1).
492. Ringland, J. (2007, 13–20 Mar). *An Information Systems Analysis of Mind, Knowledge, 'the World' and Holistic Science.* (Http://www.anandavala.info/TASTMOTNOR/InformationSystemA nalysis.html)
493. Riolo, R. L., Cohen, M. D., & Axelrod, R. (2001, 22 Nov). Evolution of cooperation without reciprocity. *Nature, 414*(6862), 441–443. (Http://www.nature.com/nature/journal/v414/n6862/pdf/414441 a0.pdf)
494. Roach, S. R. (2013). Effectively Using Interest-Based Negotiationin the Cross-Cultural Context. In *Cross Cultural Negotiations for US Negotiators.*
495. Robins, R. W. (2005, 7 Oct). The Nature of Personality: Genes, Culture, and National Character. *Science, 310*(5745), 62–63. (Http://www.sciencemag.org/cgi/reprint/310/5745/62.pdf)
496. Rockenbach, B., & Milinski, M. (2009, 1 Jan). How to Treat Those of Ill Repute. *Nature, 457*(7225), 39–40. (Http://www.nature.com/nature/journal/v457/n7225/pdf/457039 a.pdf)

497. Rosen, J. (2010, 25 Jul). The End of Forgetting. *The New York Times Magazine.*
(Http://www.nytimes.com/2010/07/25/magazine/25privacy-t2.html?_r=1&pagewanted=all)
498. Roy Luria, N. M. (2005, Oct). Increased Control Demand Results in Serial Processing. *Psychological Science, 16*(10), 833–840. (Http://www3.interscience.wiley.com/cgi-bin/fulltext/118661668/PDFSTART)
499. Rudman, L., & Phelan, J. (2007–12–01). The Interpersonal Power of Feminism: Is Feminism Good for Romantic Relationships? *Sex Roles, 57*(11), 787–799. Springer Netherlands.
500. Ruff, C. C., KristjÃinsson, Ã., & Driver, J. (2007, 1 Oct). Readout From Iconic Memory and Selective Spatial Attention Involve Similar Neural Processes. *Psychological Science, 18*(10), 901–909.
(Http://pss.sagepub.com/content/18/10/901.full.pdf+html)
501. Rule, N. O., Ambady, N., & Hallett, K. C. (2009, Nov). Female sexual orientation is perceived accurately, rapidly, and automatically from the face and its features. *Journal of Experimental Social Psychology, 45*(6), 1245–1251.
(Http://www.sciencedirect.com/science?_ob=MImg&_imagekey=B6WJB-4WVF6W2-1-7&_cdi=6874&_user=10&_orig=search&_coverDate=11%2F30%2F2009&_sk=999549993&view=c&wchp=dGLzVlz-zSkWb&md5=1e560928c3a34ba2cb43df6195b7a251&ie=/sdarticle.pdf)
502. Rustagi, D., Engel, S., & Kosfeld, M. (2010, 12 Nov). Conditional Cooperation and Costly Monitoring Explain Success in Forest Commons Management. *Science, 330*(6006), 961–965. (Http://www.sciencemag.org/content/330/6006/961.full.pdf)
503. Saalmann, Y. B., Pinsk, M. A., Wang, L., Li, X., & Kastner, S. (2012, 10 Aug). The Pulvinar Regulates Information Transmission Between Cortical Areas Based on Attention Demands. *Science, 337*(6095), 753–756.
(Http://www.sciencemag.org/content/337/6095/753.full.pdf)

504. Sakaiya, T. (1991). *The knowledge-value revolution, or, A history of the future.* Tokyo ; New York: Kodansha International: Distributed in the U.S. by Kodansha America. (Http://www.amazon.com/gp/product/0870119427/sr=1-1/qid=1295217319/ref=olp_product_details/185-7849946-8512265?ie=UTF8&me=&qid=1295217319&sr=1-1&seller=)
505. Salazar, R. F., Dotson, N. M., Bressler, S. L., & Gray, C. M. (2012, 23 Nov). Content-Specific Fronto-Parietal Synchronization During Visual Working Memory. *Science, 338*(6110), 1097–1100. (Http://www.sciencemag.org/content/338/6110/1097.full)
506. Sanchez, D., Moss-Racusin, C., Phelan, J., & Crocker, J. (2011-02-01). Relationship Contingency and Sexual Motivation in Women: Implications for Sexual Satisfaction. *Archives of Sexual Behavior, 40*(1), 99–110. Springer Netherlands.
507. Sandberg, A., & Soderberg, R. (1997). Computer Generation: Visions and Demands. Military Applications of Synthetic Environments and Virtual Reality, MASERV'97. Sweden.
508. Sandra Graham. (2006). Peer Victimization in School: Exploring the Ethnic Context. *Current Directions in Psychological Science, 15*(6), 317–321. (Http://www3.interscience.wiley.com/cgi-bin/fulltext/118584122/PDFSTART)
509. Sanfey, A. G., Rilling, J. K., Aronson, J. A., Nystrom, L. E., & Cohen, J. D. (2003, 13 Jun). The Neural Basis of Economic Decision-Making in the Ultimatum Game. *Science, 300*(5626), 1755–1758. (Http://www.sciencemag.org/cgi/reprint/sci;300/5626/1755.pdf)
510. Scheibert, J., Leurent, S., Prevost, A., & Debregeas, G. (2009, 13 Mar). The Role of Fingerprints in the Coding of Tactile Information Probed with a Biomimetic Sensor. *Science, 323*(5920), 1503–1506. (Http://www.sciencemag.org/cgi/reprint/sci;323/5920/1503.pdf)
511. Schick, A., Wessa, M., Vollmayr, B., Kuehner, C., & Kanske, P. (2013, 12 Jun). Indirect assessment of an interpretation bias in humans: Neurophysiological and behavioral correlates. *Frontiers in Human Neuroscience, 7.* (Http://www.frontiersin.org/Journal/DownloadFile.ashx?pdf=1&Fil

eId=257340&articleId=44420&Version=1&ContentTypeId=21&Fil
eName=fnhum-07–00272.pdf)
512. Schindler, V. M., & Cler, M. (2007). *Cultural Identity and
Color Communication in Urban Space and Contemporary
Architecture.* Paris.
513. Schmidt, C., Collette, F., Leclercq, Y., Sterpenich, V.,
Vandewalle, G., Berthomier, P., et al. (2009, 24 Apr).
Homeostatic Sleep Pressure and Responses to Sustained
Attention in the Suprachiasmatic Area. *Science, 324*(5926), 516–
519. (Http://www.sciencemag.org/cgi/reprint/324/5926/516.pdf)
514. Schnegg, M. (2006). *Reciprocity and the Emergence of
Power Laws in Social Networks.* CERN: CERN Document Server.
(Http://cdsweb.cern.ch/record/932828?ln=en)
515. Schultz, T. F., & Kay, S. A. (2003, 18 Jul). Circadian Clocks
in Daily and Seasonal Control of Development.
Science, 301(5631), 326–328.
(Http://www.sciencemag.org/cgi/reprint/sci;301/5631/326.pdf)
516. Schuster, D., & Undreiu, A. Cognition of an expert tackling
an unfamiliar conceptual physics problem. Michigan State
University; University of Michigan;.
(Http://physics2.sciencecommunity.wikispaces.net/file/view/cogn
ition+of+an+expert+tackling+an+unfamiliar+problem.pdf)
517. Schwartz, A. B., Moran, D. W., & Reina, G. A. (2004, 16
Jan). Differential Representation of Perception and Action in the
Frontal Cortex. *Science, 303*(5656), 380–383.
(Http://www.sciencemag.org/cgi/reprint/303/5656/380.pdf)
518. Schwartz, H., Eichstaedt, J., Dziurzynski, L., & Ramones, S.
(2013, 25 Sep). Personality, Gender, and Age in the Language of
Social Media: The Open-Vocabulary Approach. *PLoS One, 8*(9).
(Http://www.plosone.org/article/fetchObject.action;jsessionid=53
74E28E1A87A4693F166ACB2915DD41?uri=info%3Adoi%2F10.13
71%2Fjournal.pone.0073791&representation=PDF)
519. Schwartz, J. (2007, 23 Jan). *IPhone Seeds Mobile Marketing
Growth.* IMediaConnection.
(Http://www.imediaconnection.com/content/13331.asp)
520. Seabright, P. (2004). *The Company of Strangers : A Natural
History of Economic Life.* Princeton: Princeton University Press.

521. Seidenberg, M. S., Elman, J. L., Negishi, M., Eimas, et al. (1999, 16 Apr). Rule Learning by Seven-Month-Old Infants (Do Infants Learn Grammar with Algebra or Statistics?). *Science, 284*(5413), 433. (Http://www.sciencemag.org/cgi/content/full/284/5413/433f)

522. Seife, C. (2003, 8 Aug). 'Terrorism Futures' Could Have a Future, Experts Say. *Science, 301*(5634). (Http://www.sciencemag.org/cgi/reprint/sci;301/5634/749.pdf)

523. Senghas, A., Kita, S., & Ozyurek, A. (2004, 17 Sep). Children Creating Core Properties of Language: Evidence from an Emerging Sign Language in Nicaragua. *Science, 305*(5691), 1779–1782. (Http://www.sciencemag.org/cgi/reprint/305/5691/1779.pdf)

524. Shaikh, A. D., Chaparro, B. S., & Fox, D. (2009, Oct). The Personality of Terms and Concepts Used in Online Material. *Usability News (Software Usability Research Laboratory (SURL) at Wichita State University), 11*(1). (Http://www.surl.org/usabilitynews/111/pdf/Usability%20News%20111%20-%20Shaikh.pdf)

525. Shaikh, A. D., Chaparro, B. S., Nelson, W. T., & Joshi, A. (2005, Feb). Metaphors and Website Design: A Cross-Cultural Case Study of the Tide.com Stain Detective. *Usability News (Software Usability Research Laboratory (SURL) at Wichita State University), 7*(1). (Http://www.surl.org/usabilitynews/71/pdf/Usability%20News%2071%20-%20Shaikh.pdf)

526. Shariff, A. F., & Norenzayan, A. (2007, 1 Sep). God Is Watching You. *Psychological Science, 18*(9), 803–809. (Http://pss.sagepub.com/content/18/9/803.full.pdf+html)

527. Shena Lu. (2006, Feb). Cue Duration and Parvocellular Guidance of Visual Attention. *Psychological Science, 17*(2), 101–102. (Http://www3.interscience.wiley.com/cgi-bin/fulltext/118597326/PDFSTART)

528. Sherratt, T. N., & Roberts, G. (2012, 14 Sep). When Paths to Cooperation Converge. *Science, 337*(6100), 1304–1305. (Http://www.sciencemag.org/content/337/6100/1304.full.pdf)

529. Shneiderman, B., & Preece, J. (2007, 16 Feb). 911,gov. *Science, 315.* (Http://www.sciencemag.org/content/315/5814/944.full.pdf)
530. Shumake, J., Ilango, A., Scheich, H., Wetzel, W., & Ohl, F. W. (2010, 28 Apr). Differential Neuromodulation of Acquisition and Retrieval of Avoidance Learning by the Lateral Habenula and Ventral Tegmental Area. *The Journal of Neuroscience, 30*(17), 5876–5883. (Http://www.jneurosci.org/content/30/17/5876.full.pdf+html)
531. Siegel, D. (2010, Nov). Competition in Large and Small Groups. *APS Observer, 23.* (Http://www.psychologicalscience.org/index.php/publications/observer/2010/november-10/vying-for-the-prize-competition-in-large-and-small-groups.html)
532. Sievers, B., Polansky, L., Casey, M., & Wheatley, T. (2013, 2 Jan). Music and movement share a dynamic structure that supports universal expressions of emotion. *Proceedings of the National Academy of Sciences, 110*(1), 70–75.
533. Sigmund, K., De Silva, H., Traulsen, A., & Hauert, C. (2010, 12 Aug). Social learning promotes institutions for governing the commons. *Nature, 466*(7308), 861–863. (Http://www.nature.com/nature/journal/v466/n7308/pdf/nature09203.pdf)
534. Sigmund, K., Fehr, E., & Nowak, M. A. The Economics of Fair Play. *Scientific American.*
535. Sigmund, K., & Nowak, M. A. (2001, 22 Nov). Tides of tolerance. *Nature, 414*(6862), 403–405. (Http://www.nature.com/nature/journal/v414/n6862/pdf/414403a0.pdf)
536. Silk, J. B., Brosnan, S. F., Vonk, J., Henrich, J., Povinelli, D. J., Richardson, A. S., et al. (2005, 27 Oct). Chimpanzees are indifferent to the welfare of unrelated group members. *Nature, 437*(7063), 1357–1359. (Http://www.nature.com/nature/journal/v437/n7063/pdf/nature04243.pdf)
537. Silk, J. B. (2006, 3 March). Who Are More Helpful, Humans or Chimpanzees? *Science, 311,* 1248–1249.

538. Sinatra, R., Moreno, Y., Gómez-Gardeñes, J. ú., Latora, V., & Floría, L. M. (2008). *The emergence and structure of altruism in social networks.* CERN: CERN Document Server. (Http://cdsweb.cern.ch/record/1113909)

539. Sinervo, B., & Clobert, J. (2003, 20 Jun). Morphs, Dispersal Behavior, Genetic Similarity, and the Evolution of Cooperation. *Science, 300*(5627), 1949–1951.

540. Sleek, S. (2016, Feb). Love in the Time of Twitter. *APS Observer, 29.* (Http://www.psychologicalscience.org/index.php/publications/observer/2016/february-16/love-in-the-time-of-twitter.html)

541. Smith, A. (2009, Oct). Pushing the Right Buttons: Design Characteristics of Touch Screen Buttons. *Usability News (Software Usability Research Laboratory (SURL) at Wichita State University), 11*(2). (Http://www.surl.org/usabilitynews/112/pdf/Usability%20News%20112%20-%20Smith.pdf)

542. Smith, B. (2012, 21 Jun). Complexities of flavour. *Nature, 486*(7403), S6-S6. (Http://www.nature.com/nature/journal/v486/n7403_supp/pdf/486S6a.pdf)

543. Smythies, J. (2009). Philosophy, Perception and Neuroscience. *Perception, 38*(5).

544. Snyder, M. (1987). *Public Appearances, Private Realities.* NYC: W.H. Freeman and Company.

545. Sosulski, D. L., Lissitsyna Bloom, M., Cutforth, T., Axel, R., & Datta, S. R. (2011, 14 Apr). Distinct representations of olfactory information in different cortical centres. *Nature, 472*(7342), 213–216.

546. Sources and Resources. (2011, May). *Evidence & Policy: A Journal of Research, Debate and Practice, 7*(2), 227–244.

547. Sparrow, B., Liu, J., & Wegner, D. M. (2011, 5 Aug). Google Effects on Memory: Cognitive Consequences of Having Information at Our Fingertips. *Science, 333*(6043), 776–778. (Http://www.sciencemag.org/content/333/6043/776.full.pdf)

548. Spielberg, J. M., Heller, W., & Miller, G. A. (2013, 17 Jun). Hierarchical brain networks active in approach and avoidance goal

pursuit. *Frontiers in Human Neuroscience, 7.*
(Http://www.frontiersin.org/Journal/DownloadFile.ashx?pdf=1&Fil
eId=262222&articleId=51032&Version=1&ContentTypeId=21&Fil
eName=fnhum-07–00284.pdf)
549. Steckenfinger, S. A., & Ghazanfar, A. A. (2009, 27 Oct).
Monkey visual behavior falls into the uncanny valley. *Proceedings
of the National Academy of Sciences, 106*(43), 18362–18366.
(Http://www.pnas.org/content/106/43/18362.full.pdf+html)
550. Stephenson, K., Ahrold, T., & Meston, C. (2011–06–01). The
Association Between Sexual Motives and Sexual Satisfaction:
Gender Differences and Categorical Comparisons. *Archives of
Sexual Behavior, 40*(3), 607–618. Springer Netherlands.
551. Stone, R. (2009, 26 Jun). China Reins in Wilder Impulses in
Treatment of 'Internet Addiction.' *Science, 324.*
552. Storm, B. C., & Stone, S. M. (2015, 1 Feb). Saving-
Enhanced Memory: The Benefits of Saving on the Learning and
Remembering of New Information. *Psychological
Science, 26*(2), 182 -188.
553. Suchak, M., & de Waal, F. B. M. (2012, 18 Sep). Monkeys
benefit from reciprocity without the cognitive burden. *Proceedings
of the National Academy of Sciences, 109*(38), 15191–15196.
(Http://www.pnas.org/content/109/38/15191.full.pdf+html)
554. Sugrue, L. P., Corrado, G. S., & Newsome, W. T. (2004, 18
June). Matching Behavior and the Representation of Value in the
Parietal Cortex. *Science, 304*(5678), 1782–1787.
(Http://www.sciencemag.org/cgi/reprint/sci;304/5678/1782.pdf)
555. Surel, D. (2011, Jan-Mar). Speaking from the Heart.
EdgeScience, 6.
556. Swan, A., Cockerill, M., & Sipp, D. (2013/03/28/).
Advocacy: How to hasten open access. *Nature, 495*(7442), 442–
443.
(Http://www.nature.com/nature/journal/v495/n7442/full/495442
a.html)
557. Szolnoki, A., & Perc, M. (2010). *Reward and cooperation in
the spatial public goods game.* EconoPhysics Forum.
(Http://www.unifr.ch/econophysics/paper/download/id/1010.577
1/format/pdf)

558. Tan, J., Ma, Z., Gao, X., Wu, Y., & Fang, F. (2011, 24 May). Gender Difference of Unconscious Attentional Bias in High Trait Anxiety Individuals. *PLoS ONE, 6*(5).

559. Tang, T. Z., DeRubeis, R. J., Hollon, S. D., Amsterdam, J., Shelton, R., & Schalet, B. (2009, 1 Dec). Personality Change During Depression Treatment: A Placebo-Controlled Trial. *Arch Gen Psychiatry, 66*(12), 1322–1330. (Http://archpsyc.ama-assn.org/cgi/reprint/66/12/1322)

560. Tania Singer, & Nikolaus Steinbeis. (2009). Differential Roles of Fairness- and Compassion-Based Motivations for Cooperation, Defection, and Punishment. *Annals of the New York Academy of Sciences, 1167*(Values, Empathy, and Fairness across Social Barriers), 41–50. (Http://www3.interscience.wiley.com/cgi-bin/fulltext/122466375/PDFSTART)

561. Taylor, P. D., Day, T., & Wild, G. (2007, 24 May). Evolution of cooperation in a finite homogeneous graph. *Nature, 447,* 469–472. (Http://www.nature.com/nature/journal/v447/n7143/pdf/nature05784.pdf)

562. Tehrani, J. (2013, Nov). The Phylogeny of Little Red Riding Hood. *PLoS ONE, 8*(11). (Http://www.plosone.org/article/fetchObject.action;jsessionid=47299A48708D7BEE970A441BA16E9779?uri=info%3Adoi%2F10.1371%2Fjournal.pone.0078871&representation=PDF)

563. Telis, & Gisela. (2009, 9 Apr). *What You See Is What You Feel.* ScienceNow Daily News. (Http://sciencenow.sciencemag.org/cgi/content/full/2009/409/1?twitter=1)

564. ter Bogt, T., Engels, R., Bogers, S., & Kloosterman, M. (2010-12-01). "Shake It Baby, Shake It": Media Preferences, Sexual Attitudes and Gender Stereotypes Among Adolescents. *Sex Roles, 63*(11), 844–859. Springer Netherlands.

565. Terracciano, A., Abdel-Khalek, A. M., Adam, N., Adamovova, L., Ahn, C.-k., Ahn, H.-n., et al. (2005, 7 Oct). National Character Does Not Reflect Mean Personality Trait Levels in 49 Cultures.

Science, 310(5745), 96–100.
(Http://www.sciencemag.org/cgi/reprint/310/5745/96.pdf)
566. Thompson, K. G., Biscoe, K. L., & Sato, T. R. (2005, 12 Oct).
Neuronal Basis of Covert Spatial Attention in the Frontal Eye
Field. *Journal of Neuroscience, 25*(41), 9479–9487.
(Http://www.jneurosci.org/cgi/reprint/25/41/9479)
567. Tis the Season for Giving. (2012, Dec). *APS Observer, 25.*
(Http://www.psychologicalscience.org/index.php/publications/obs
erver/2012/december-12/tis-the-season-for-giving.html)
568. Tom, S. M., Fox, C. R., Trepel, C., & Poldrack, R. A. (2007,
26 Jan). The Neural Basis of Loss Aversion in Decision-Making
Under Risk. *Science, 315,* 515–518.
(Http://www.sciencemag.org/cgi/reprint/315/5811/515.pdf)
569. Tomasello, M., & Warneken, F. (2008, 28 Aug). Share and
share alike. *Nature, 454*(7208), 1057–1058.
570. Topal, J., Gergely, G., Erdohegyi, A., Csibra, G., & Miklosi, A.
(2009, 4 Sep). Differential Sensitivity to Human Communication
in Dogs, Wolves, and Human Infants. *Science, 325*(5945), 1269–
1272.
(Http://www.sciencemag.org/cgi/reprint/325/5945/1269.pdf)
571. Townsend JM, & Wasserman T. (1997, Jun). The perception
of sexual attractiveness: Sex differences in variability. *Archives of
Sexual Behavior, 26*(3), 243–68.
572. Travis, J. (1996, 17 Feb). Biological stopwatch found in the
brain. *Science News, 149,* 7.
573. Tsao, D. (2006, 6 Oct). A Dedicated System for Processing
Faces. *Science, 314.*
574. Tuan, Y.-F. (1977). *Space and Place.* Minneapolis: University
of Minnesota Press.
575. Tuan, Y.-F. (1979). *Landscapes of Fear.* University of
Minnesota Press.
576. Ule, A., Schram, A., Riedl, A., & Cason, T. N. (2009, 18
Dec). Indirect Punishment and Generosity Toward Strangers.
Science, 326(5960), 1701–1704.
(Http://www.sciencemag.org/cgi/reprint/sci;326/5960/1701.pdf)

577. Umberto Romani, & Giovanni Tondini. (2005, 1 Mar). M.L. Weitzman vs J.M. Buchanan. *Int J of Social Economics, 32*(1/2), 5–16.
578. Vaidhyanathan, S. (2011, June). Protecting Online Privacy. *ieee Spectrum.* (Http://spectrum.ieee.org/telecom/internet/protecting-online-privacy/0)
579. Vallesi A., Binns M., & Shallice T. (2008). An effect of spatial-temporal association of response codes: Understanding the cognitive representations of time. *Cognition, 107*(2), 501–527.
580. VanBoskirk, S. (2005). *Integrated Marketing Grows Up.* Forrester Research.
581. Vandenbroucke, S., Crombez, G., Van Ryckeghem, D., Brass, M., Van Damme, S., & Goubert, L. (2013, 11 Jun). Vicarious pain experiences while observing another in pain: An experimental approach. *Frontiers in Human Neuroscience, 7.* (Http://www.frontiersin.org/Journal/DownloadFile.ashx?pdf=1&FileId=255965&articleId=47526&Version=1&ContentTypeId=21&FileName=fnhum-07-00265.pdf)
582. Vannini, P. (2002, June). Waiting Dynamics: Bergson, Virilio, Deleuze, and the Experience of Global Times. *Journal of Mundane Behavior, 3*(2).
583. Vaughn, J. E., Bradley, K. I., Byrd-Craven, J., & Kennison, S. M. (2010, Sep). The Effect of Mortality Salience on Women's Judgments of Male Faces. *Evolutionary Psychology, 8*(3), 477–491. (Http://www.epjournal.net/filestore/EP07477491.pdf?utm_source=MadMimi&utm_medium=email&utm_content=September+2010+Newsletter&utm_campaign=September+2010+Newsletter&utm_term=The%2Beffect%2Bof%2Bmortality%2Bsalience%2Bon%2Bwomen_E2_80_99s%2Bjudgments%2Bof%2Bmale%2Bfaces_)
584. Vlok, D. (2005). An Assessment of the Knowledge Processing Environment in an Organisation - A Case Study. Rhodes Investec Business School: Rhodes University. (Www.macroinnovation.com/Assessment_of_Knowledge_Processing.pdf)

585. Vogel, G. (2004, 20 Feb). The Evolution of the Golden Rule. *Science, 303*(5661), 1128–1131.
(Http://www.sciencemag.org/cgi/reprint/sci;303/5661/1128.pdf)
586. Vohs, K. D., Mead, N. L., & Goode, M. R. (2006, 17 Nov). The Psychological Consequences of Money.
Science, 314(5802), 1154–1156.
(Http://www.sciencemag.org/content/314/5802/1154.full.pdf)
587. Volk, A. A., Darrell-Cheng, C., & Marini, Z. A. (2010, Oct). Paternal Care May Influence Perceptions of Paternal Resemblance. *Evolutionary Psychology.*
(Http://www.epjournal.net/filestore/EP08516529.pdf)
588. Vollan, B., & Ostrom, E. (2010, 12 Nov). Cooperation and the Commons. *Science, 330*(6006), 923–924.
(Http://www.sciencemag.org/content/330/6006/923.full.pdf)
589. Voss, A., & Procter, R. (2009). Virtual research environments in scholarly work and communications. *Library Hi Tech, 27*(2), 174–190.
590. Waibel, M., Floreano, D., & Keller, L. (2011, 3 May). A Quantitative Test of Hamilton's Rule for the Evolution of Altruism. *PLoS Biol, 9*(5).
(Http://www.plosbiology.org/article/fetchObjectAttachment.action ?uri=info%3Adoi%2F10.1371%2Fjournal.pbio.1000615&represen tation=PDF)
591. Wald, C. (2008, 12 Dec). Crazy Money. *Science, 322.*
592. Wallis, & Walters. (2015, 19 May). The Power of Sharing Linked Data: Giving the Web What It Wants. *The Serials Librarian, 68*(s 1–4), 173–179.
593. Walter, F., Battiston, S., & Schweitzer, F. (2008, 1 Feb). A model of a trust-based recommendation system on a social network. *Autonomous Agents and Multi-Agent Systems, 16*(1), 57–74.
(Http://www.springerlink.com/content/yp94v7553p322072/fullte xt.pdf)
594. Wan, X., Nakatani, H., Ueno, K., Asamizuya, T., Cheng, K., & Tanaka, K. (2011, 21 Jan). The Neural Basis of Intuitive Best Next-Move Generation in Board Game Experts.

Science, 331(6015), 341–346.
(Http://www.sciencemag.org/content/331/6015/341.full.pdf)
595. Wang, J., & Lim, A. (2009). Local touch and global reach:
The next generation of network-level information discovery and
delivery services in a digital landscape. *Library Management, 30*(s
1–2), 25–34.
596. Wang, S. (2013). Tit for Tat in the Global Perspective. In
Cross Cultural Negotiations for US Negotiators.
597. Warneken, F., & Tomasello, M. (2006, 3 March). Altruistic
Helping in Human Infants and Young Chimpanzees.
Science, 311, 1301–1303.
598. Watts, D. J., Dodds, P. S., & Newman, M. E. J. (2002, 17
May). Identity and Search in Social Networks.
Science, 296(5571), 1302–1305.
(Http://www.sciencemag.org/cgi/reprint/296/5571/1302.pdf)
599. Waxman, S. R., & Lidz, J. Early Word learning. In *Handbook
of Child Psychology.*
600. Webster, M. A., Kaping, D., Mizokami, Y., & Duhamel, P.
(2004, 1 Apr). Adaptation to natural facial categories.
Nature, 428(6982), 557–561.
(Http://www.nature.com/nature/journal/v428/n6982/pdf/nature0
2420.pdf)
601. *WebTrends SmartSource Data Management: Premier Client-
Side Data Collection Technology White Paper.* (2003). NetIQ.
602. Wedekind, C., & Milinski, M. (2000, 5 May). Cooperation
Through Image Scoring in Humans. *Science, 288*(5467), 850–
852.
(Https://www.sciencemag.org/cgi/reprint/sci;288/5467/850.pdf)
603. Weikum, W. M., Vouloumanos, A., Navarra, J., Soto-Faraco,
S., Sebastian-Galles, N., & Werker, J. F. (2007, 25 May). Visual
Language Discrimination in Infancy. *Science, 316,* 1159.
(Http://www.sciencemag.org/cgi/reprint/316/5828/1159.pdf)
604. West, S. A., & Gardner, A. (2010, 12 Mar). Altruism, Spite,
and Greenbeards. *Science, 327*(5971), 1341–1344.
(Http://www.sciencemag.org/content/327/5971/1341.full.pdf)
605. West, S. A., Pen, I., & Griffin, A. S. (2002, 5 Apr).
Cooperation and Competition Between Relatives.

Science, 296(5565), 72–75.
(Http://www.sciencemag.org/cgi/reprint/sci;296/5565/72.pdf)
606. Whalen, P. J., Kagan, J., Cook, R. G., Davis, F. C., Kim, H.,
Polis, S., et al. (2004, 17 Dec). Human Amygdala Responsivity to
Masked Fearful Eye Whites. *Science, 306*(5704).
(Http://www.sciencemag.org/cgi/reprint/306/5704/2061.pdf)
607. Where objects go in the brain. (1995, 16 Sep). *Science
News.*
(Http://www.thefreelibrary.com/Where+objects+go+in+the+brai
n.-a017495093)
608. White, G. (2007). Broadening participation - the future of
resource discovery. *Interlending & Document Supply, 35*(1), 28–
30.
609. Whitfield, J. (2002, 19 Sep). Nosy neighbours.
Nature, 419(6904), 242–243.
(Http://www.nature.com/nature/journal/v419/n6904/pdf/419242
a.pdf)
610. Wierzbicka, A. (1999). *Emotions Across Language and
Cultures.* Cambridge University: Cambridge University Press.
611. Williams, D. (2004). Trouble in River City: The Social Life of
VIDEO Games. University of Michigan.
612. Winchester, M., & Romaniuk, J. (2001, 5 Dec). Do Negative
Brand Image Attributes Display Evaluative and Descriptive
Patterns? Australian and New Zealand Marketing Academy.
Massey University, Auckland, NZ.
(Http://smib.vuw.ac.nz:8081/WWW/ANZMAC2001/anzmac/AUTH
ORS/pdfs/Winchester.pdf)
613. Winerman, L. (2009, 22 Jan). Crisis Communication.
Nature, 457(7228), 376–378.
(Http://www.nature.com/news/2009/090121/pdf/457376a.pdf)
614. Wynne, C. D. L. (2004, 11 Mar). Animal behaviour: Fair
refusal by capuchin monkeys. *Nature, 428*(6979), 140–140.
(Http://www.nature.com/nature/journal/v428/n6979/pdf/428140
a.pdf)
615. Yair Bar-Haim, T. Z., Dominique Lamy. (2006, Feb). Nature
and Nurture in Own-Race Face Processing. *Psychological
Science, 17*(2), 159–163.

(Http://www3.interscience.wiley.com/cgi-
bin/fulltext/118597334/PDFSTART)
616. Yamagishi, T., Hashimoto, H., & Schug, J. (2008, 1 Jun).
Preferences Versus Strategies as Explanations for Culture-Specific
Behavior. *Psychological Science, 19*(6), 579–584.
(Http://pss.sagepub.com/content/19/6/579.full.pdf+html)
617. Yu, A. J., & Dayan, P. (2005, 19 May). Uncertainty,
Neuromodulation, and Attention. *Neuron, 46*(4), 681–692.
(Http://download.cell.com/neuron/pdf/PIIS0896627305003624.p
df)
618. Zabet, F.-D. (2012). Playing Together And Ritualisation In
Online Games. Cantebury: Kent.
619. Zahay, D., Mason, C. H., & Schibrowsky, J. A. (2009, Fall).
The Present and Future of IMC and Database Marketing.
*International Journal of Integrated Marketing
Communications, 1*(2), 13–31.
620. Zangaladze, A., Epstein, C. M., Grafton, S. T., & Sathian, K.
(1999, 7 Oct). Involvement of visual cortex in tactile
discrimination of orientation. *Nature, 401*(6753), 587–590.
(Http://www.nature.com/nature/journal/v401/n6753/pdf/401587
a0.pdf)
621. Zeineh, M. M., Engel, S. A., Thompson, P. M., & Bookheimer,
S. Y. (2003, 24 Jan). Dynamics of the Hippocampus During
Encoding and Retrieval of Face-Name Pairs.
Science, 299(5606), 577–580.
(Http://www.sciencemag.org/cgi/reprint/299/5606/577.pdf)
622. Zelazniewicz, A., & Pawlowski, B. (2011, Decc). Female
breast size attractiveness for men as a function of sociosexual
orientation (restricted vs. unrestricted). *Archives of Sexual
Behavior, 40*(6), 1129–35.
623. Zelkowitz, & Rachel. (2008, 8 Dec). Dogs Have a Nose for
Inequity. *ScienceNow.*

Glossary

A

adaptation method - how the repeated action of something leads to less cognitive effort being required to perform the action

afferent - going inwards

anchoring - applying (often non-conscious) significance to some thing or event such that a psycho-cognitive, - spiritual, - emotional or -physical state can be re-experienced by simply remembering or being in the presence of the thing or event

anonymity levels - what we're not willing to let others know about us, usually demonstrated thrugh various Personalities

audience knowledgeable design - having an in-depth knowledge of your audience's psycho-cognitive, - spiritual, -emotional or -physical limits, boundaries, abilities, experiences, et cetera, and applying this knowledge to your design work

C

chinese general solicitation - a 2nd difference investigation into some desired quality. For example, if you're evaluating candidates for a high level position and all the candidates know each other, ask them individually who should get the job if something happens to the individual. Whoever gets the consensus opinion should get the job.

core - an individual's emotional, physical, spiritual and psychological center

D

digital entitlement - a sense that because I can access it I own it or have rights to it

efferent - going outwards

E

ego identification - the subsumation of an individual's own identity into some other identity to which the individual assigns greater cultural meaning

exafferent - signals external to the body that go inward. Watching TV is exafferent because there's no interaction with the information such that a change in the observer's state causes a change in the TV program's state (we're not considering changing channels because the TV show sucks)

exaptation - when one process or method that achieves one goal is co-opted to another process or method to achieve a different goal

executive function - how the brain manages cognitive processes, reasoning, the various memories, solves problems and performs solutions to problems. Executive function is also known as "the modeler", "cognitive control" and "supervisory attentional system"

F

fair-exchange - a psycho-cognitive, -emotive, -spiritual and -physical state that occurs when you give as good as you get in an exchange and all parties involved are multi-dimensionally satisfied with the exchange

I

identity - the emotional, physical, spiritual and psychological layer that exists outside the core and inside the personality. The Identity's job is to strengthen and maintain an individual's personalities while constantly protecting the Core from harm

Identity levels - what we're willing to let others know about us, usually demonstrated through various Personalities

invariant features - the elements of a system that do not change

M

meaningful noise - anything that draws an individual's attention away from what they were focusing on to something they start focusing on when the individual doesn't want to relinquish their primary focus of attention

P

personality - the outermost layer of an individual's emotional, physical, spiritual and psychological being. The Personality is what is projected into the world to interact with others. The Personality's job is to make sure the Identity remains whole despite changes in the environment that may require modifications to the Personality itself

polarity response - two extreme and opposing states to a single event

primary modality channel - the sensory system an individual uses most often to gather information about their environment

probability solids - a multidimensional manifold that is the boundary for what can happen and what can't happenprotention - an anticipation of a future event

psychomotor behavioral cuing - the minute adjustments the brain makes to the body in response to internal and external stimuli

Q

QBist - a subjective approach to quantum theory. People who adhere a Bayesian aspect to quantum mechanical properties and events

R

reafferent - signals generated by the body that are directed towards an external object. Playing a game, online or off, is

highly reafferent because the game changes based on the
player's changes

S

semiotics - the study of signs and symbols and the relationships
they create
spatial relationships - how two or more structures are related in
space

T

temporal relationships - how two or more structures are related in
time
time-phase learning loop - the time it takes for an individual to
become desensitized to environmental information

Index

About the Author

Joseph Carrabis is Founder and Chief Research Officer of The NextStage Companies and helps clients understand how people think and react to marketing, leveraging that information to improve marketing efforts. He has been awarded patents for NextStage's Evolution Technology, creating a new, disruptive field of technology and applications. Evolution Technology allows any programmable device to understand human thought and respond accordingly.

He has designed, developed and delivered over 100 tools that analyze everything from group and individual social behaviors to product design and development to community development and monitoring to consumer psychology to resume analysis and improvement to finding compatible life-partners to personal growth to training measurement for governments, businesses and individuals worldwide.

He is a Senior Research Fellow at the University of Southern California's Annenberg Center for the Digital Future; a Senior Research Fellow and Board Advisory Member for the Society for New Communications Research; a Founder, Senior Researcher and Director of Predictive Analytics for the Center for Adaptive Solutions; a member of Scientists Without Borders; has served as Chief Neuroscience Officer and currently advises the event industry about the neuroscience of events, conferences, conventions and trainings.

Joseph has authored over 25 books, including *Reading Virtual Minds Volume I: Science and History, Reading Virtual Minds Volume II: Experience and Expectation* and *Tales 'Told Round Celestial Campfires*.

NextStage Evolution Live and Webinar Trainings

Much of the material covered in this book is available as both live and webinar trainings and classes. For that matter, there's a whole lot of stuff not covered in this book that's available as live and webinar trainings and classes.

Seriously, contact us at 603-791-4925 or info@nextstagevolution.com. Tell us what you want to learn. Chances are we already have a training on it, can modify an existing training to suit your exact needs or design a new training specific to your goals and desires.

Most frequently requested trainings can be found at http://nlb.pub/G. A training schedule is available at http://nlb.pub/I.

Comments from Live and Web Training Participants

"Put down your guard, stop thinking you know what you're doing, keep quiet, watch, learn, listen. Carrabis gave us 500 things if he gave us five and each one paid off a million fold." – St. John, NB

"We didn't know what we didn't know until working with NextStage." – Bedford, MA

"I was unprepared for the amount of learning Carrabis packed into a one-day session." – Rothesay, NB

"Of all the tips and tricks that I learned, none proved more effective than the many I received from Mr. Carrabis in regards to the tone, inflection and proper nomenclature to be used in my pitch to the client. In fact, after one specific sitting with him I was able to improve my results 500%." – Burlington, MA

"I am not exaggerating: Everybody who has trained me has been excellent, but you are the best, really." – Burlington, MA

"I've worked with Joseph for three years and still find myself surprised by his truly unique perspective and insight. At the recent iMedia Brand Summit, his workshop was a big hit— both enlightening and entertaining the participants." – Los Angeles, CA

"...seeing your insights in action (especially with the relationship website and some of your ideas on how to present copy, deal with someone who is in pain, remove blame by replacing 'your relationship' with 'the relationship' – that was really cool. ... my favorite part of the time was discussing male versus female humor. ... Considering so many advertisers use humor in their ads, this is a super relevant subject." – NYC

"Ever since I met Joseph several years ago I was always fascinated by his ability to be so attentive to one's thoughts, emotions and physical messages. Since I do more speaking appearances and often meet with executives, I asked if he could coach me a little. The experience was revealing - it allowed me to uncover little things that will help me improve my verbal and non-verbal communication skills and even become more aware of others." – Stephane Hamel, Director of Innovation, Cardinal Path

"I've been lucky enough to have experienced one of the intensive individual trainings and it was simply mind-blowing/life-altering/universe-opening." – Dan Linton, Group Director Analytics at MRM // McCann

"An excellent investment of time. Joseph not only provided "how to interpret" but also gives actionable advice on 'how to respond'." – June Li, Managing Director, ClickInsight - Online Marketing Optimization Consulting

"This was a fabulous session with Joseph and the team on the moves that matter." – Dr. Amy Price, CEO at Empower2Go

"WOW, what an impressive webinar, thanks so much for opening the door, the cheek and the conversation. If you haven't had the pleasure of spending sometime with Joseph, you should start today. Different levels of information that fit just about every level of interaction. Take some time out and see if there is any room in his future classes well worth the time and energy plus you walk away ready to take on every level of interaction with a new approach. A must for businesspeople wanting to better understand the emotions and subliminal references from their perspective business relationships." – Spencer Wade, Trusted Digital Media Adviser, Google Partner, Google Partners Ambassador, City Expert

"Impressive, informative content presented to our group of volunteers in an interactive approach. Each attendee brought a different perspective on how we were reading Joseph's facial expressions and hand gestures while exhibiting traits of our personality.

"By interpreting and better understanding the behavioral patterns encountered in business settings, we learned how to generate better outcomes by counteracting with different measures overseen in the training session.

"Joseph was great! We had lots of fun practicing in real time using a new set of tools to influence whoever we were interacting with by modifying our hand gestures and facial expressions. We all enjoyed our time together sharing thoughts and perceptions on issues encountered in our everyday life.

"Each of us will definitely perform and achieve better results. Thanks Joseph and each participant in our training session." – Lyn Demers, Business Development, Product Development, E-Marketing Strategies, CHINA LOGISTICS

"My 'Know how someone is thinking' training with Joseph and Susan was life altering. A year ago, I embarked on 'the journey' with them for two days in a conference room in New Hampshire. The training focused on them observing me, me observing them, and me observing myself. Through the repetition of observations they put the information into my 'deep memory'. After which, and for about two weeks, my brain underwent a process that literally 'hurt'. Thankfully, after that period, my brain continued to work on it subconsciously and with no pain.

"I was initially concerned I wouldn't remember what I'd learned, but to my delight, a year later, I've noticed that I'm even more skilled at reading people's micro-expressions than I was immediately after the training. I have used the knowledge and new brain wiring I have in various circumstances to my advantage; be it new business pitches, presentations to large and small audiences, negotiations with clients, management of my staff, as well as general interpersonal relationships.

"Knowing what they are thinking allows me to tailor myself and my communication to the needs of the situation be it putting someone at ease, or putting myself in a position of authority. I would and have, recommended this to anyone in a leadership, management or a sales position." – Shaina Boone, Managing Director, Marketing Decision Sciences at OMD USA

Contact Northern Lights Publishing

Did you enjoy Joseph Carrabis' *Reading Virtual Minds Volume III: Fair-Exchange and Social Networks*? We hope so and would be interested in your thoughts on what worked and what didn't, and if you'd be interested in reading anything else by Joseph Carrabis or some of our other authors.

Other Northern Lights Books include:

Consumer Science:
Reading Virtual Minds Volume I: Science and History
*Reading Virtual Minds Volume II: Experience and
        Expectation*

Fiction:
Empty Sky
Tales Told Round Celestial Campfires

You can email us with your comments at feedback@northernlightspublishing.com.

---

[a] — http://nlb.pub/jdcamazon

www.ingramcontent.com/pod-product-compliance
Lightning Source LLC
Chambersburg PA
CBHW071051280326
41928CB00050B/2203